THIS BOOK TELLS YOU

- How to do it *on your own*, without heavy packs or expensive tours.

- How to do it *at your own pace*, regardless of age or background.

- How to do it *at a cost so low* you can go back again ... and again.

Practical details shared by one who has walked and loved and inquired....

I saved $200 on train fares, B&B and postage alone.

...Knowledge gleaned from twenty years of slow rambling and fast thinking.

Books by Richard Hayward

BRITISH FOOTPATH HANDBOOK
Independent Walking Tours of England, Wales & Scotland

BRITISH FOOTPATH BIBLIOGRAPHY
Annotated Guide to Guidebooks

BRITISH FOOTPATH SAMPLER
28 Favorite Day Walks & 12 *Easy* Long Distance Paths

THE COTSWOLD WAY
A Walk Through Middle-Earth

COAST TO COAST WALK
A Serendipitous Journey Across England

CORNWALL COAST PATH GUIDE
Lands End to Lizard Point

PILGRIM'S WAY GUIDE
A Week's Walk in Kent

HADRIAN'S WALL WALK GUIDE
A Journey Through Time

THREE DALES WAY GUIDE
Buttercups and Drystone Walls

PEMBROKESHIRE COAST PATH GUIDE
Of Dragons and Wildflowers

ISLE OF WIGHT COAST PATH GUIDE
England in Miniature

FIFE COAST PATH GUIDE
Edinburgh to St Andrews

◊

For brief descriptions of these, please see end-leaves.

British Footpath Handbook

Independent
Walking Tours
of
England, Wales & Scotland

◊

Richard Hayward

To John Hillaby, a Fellow Traveler

Text and Drawings
Copyright © 1990, 1998 by Richard Hayward

Published in the United States
by *British Footpaths*
914 Mason, Bellingham WA 98225

First Edition 1990
Second Edition 1994
Third Edition 1998

British Footpaths Logo ® by Richard Hayward
ISBN 1-880848-20-1

CONTENTS

Please Note:

*T*O WALK in Britain is to explore off the beaten track and to find your day filled with small serendipities.

Imagine strolling through the English countryside along waymarked paths, meeting locals who do not treat you like a tourist, exploring Medieval castle ruins in the morning, pausing for lunch beside a Celtic burial mound, feeling the wind in your face as you stride along a Roman road, over a 500-year-old stone bridge, or beside an 18th-century canal....

Walking – which is a way of touching – is like making love to the landscape, and letting that love be returned throughout your whole being.

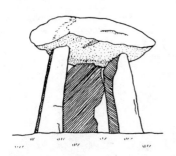

Preface

DISCOVER Britain in depth! Do it at your own pace, and at a cost so low you can't help going back. Walk from village to village along waymarked paths. Encounter Roman roads, Medieval castles, and pre-Celtic ruins. Both land and people will become your friends.

If you are an Anglophile, you have just discovered a uniquely intimate way to explore the green and pleasant land of your waking dreams.

If you are a hiker or a backpacker accustomed to the rigors of the Appalachians or the majesty of the Cascades, you may want to change gears, and boots.

If you are a budget traveler, you've just found a way to go, and go back (again, and again!) – without mortgaging your best friend or quitting your job.

A Gardener? Tree-lover? Birdwatcher? Pub-crawler? Mushroom picker? Train-spotter? Geographer? Geologist? Historian?... You've found a way to pursue your passion and expand your sympathies at the same time.

In a specialized world that rewards adults for knowing more and more about less and less ... British footpaths invite us to become children again. To see the world as interconnected and whole. To be curious and playful, to laugh and cry. To open ourselves to the new. To greet the unfamiliar not as an enemy, but as a friend and teacher.

Most of all, British footpaths remind us that we are not only professors and plumbers, secretaries and salesmen. We are also human beings – each with an astonishing array of personal experience and a unique way of understanding the world.

You have a joyful adventure ahead of you.

Chapter 1

WHY ENGLAND?

W HY GO halfway around the world to take a walk?

◊

The short answer is that walking is a national pastime in England, and a good way to meet the English people.

In England everyone walks. You will meet 85-year-olds and five-year-olds, scientists and sportsmen, teachers and builders and lovers. Class distinctions disappear on the footpath. And when you meet these people, they will not see you as a tourist, but as a fellow traveler who shares their love for the countryside.

◊

The long answer consists of two personal biases and two facts: *Beauty, History, People* and *Access.*

BEAUTY

The first bias is that Britain has the most *beautiful* countryside in the world. Rural England possesses a quality of green which, if you are susceptible, will move you deeply. Vast woodlands that once covered all of Britain have been greatly reduced over the years, revealing the curves and contours of a landscape of sensuous beauty. Also there is a human scale to the hills and valleys and rivers that makes the beauty accessible. It is not intimidating, but inviting.

◊

HISTORY

The first fact is the layers of *history* that exist in Britain. An incredible density of the stuff surrounds you in any ordinary field or village. You can follow a Roman road, stumble upon a Celtic burial mound, walk past a Napoleonic Martello Tower, pick blackberries from a Saxon hedgerow, or quaff a pint from a 13th-century pub – all in a morning's walk to the next village.

Also, England's history is not confined to museums and glass cases. It is living history, and you participate in it. Disused churches have become craft centers, theaters or government offices. Former Victorian railway lines are made into public rights-of-way. And *walking* through the countryside provides a direct connection with the earth and a powerful sense of the layers of history beneath your feet.

◊

PEOPLE

The second bias is the English *people*. Beneath their Old-World reserve I have found a humanness, an openness, a deep sense of security that enables them to laugh at themselves. A thousand years with no successful invasion has developed a sturdy sense of national and personal identity among the British.

This strong sense of identity permits them, at their best, to respond to people as being more important than regulations. The general attitude seems to be: *"For every human problem, there is a human solution."* The rulebook need be consulted only if common sense, imagination, and good humor do not produce a way out of, or around, the problem at hand.

In a world plagued by bureaucracy on one hand and Big Brother on the other, such an attitude is refreshing. If England is a corner of relative sanity in a mad world, it has something to do with this strong sense of identity, sense of humor, and belief that people are more important than rules.

ACCESS

A final point (and second fact) is that Britain has the most *accessible* countryside in the world. Let's count the ways:

1) *Friendly Climate* – Polite rain, low humidity, and no mosquitoes. It is possible to die of exposure in England, but you have to work at it.

2) *Friendly Language* – Cookies are "bikkies" and band-aids are "plasters," but the language is still recognizably our own. Most of the time we at least *think* we understand the British and (even more risky) that they understand us! But it is all great fun, and for the most part the differences are interesting rather than intimidating.

3) *Footpath Network* – Over 120,000 miles of public rights of way exist in England and Wales alone! You could walk ten miles a day for the rest of your life, and not begin to exhaust the possibilities. Only Norway and Austria have similar laws governing access to their countryside.

4) *Public Transport* – Still good despite recent cutbacks. You can get most places by bus or train, which makes the countryside accessible without a car.

5) *Frequent Villages* – Villages are often only 5 to 10 miles apart, and even closer in parts of Southern England. This makes it easy to end your day's walk in a place with food and shelter.

6) *Bed and Breakfast* – Most towns and villages have B&B, you do not normally have to book ahead, and they are affordable. B&B's thus make walking in England accessible in three ways: choice, convenience, and cost.

7) *Pubs* – Most towns and villages have at least one pub. Not only places of good cheer, companionship, and local knowledge, English pubs also serve homecooked meals at reasonable prices and sometimes provide accommodation.

8) *Lightweight Packs* – Thanks to pubs and B&B's, you don't have to carry a sleeping bag, tent, stove or food. This means your pack can weigh as little as 8 to 10 pounds.

9) *Shoes vs Boots* – Because your pack is so light, footwear becomes a question of personal taste and comfort, rather than safety or survival. With rare exceptions, ordinary shoes work fine. Some walkers even prefer "trainers" or running shoes, which are lightweight and dry quickly after rain.

10) *Youth Hostels* – Britain has excellent youth hostels. These are convenient meccas for meeting fellow walkers, and cost even less than B&B's.

11) *Public Toilets* – "Public conveniences" are readily available in towns, villages and pubs. For those with WTB's (wee tiny bladders), the countryside provides a *secludus hydrofolium* (private waterbush) every few hundred yards.

12) *Ordnance Survey Maps* – England is the best mapped country in the world. *Landrangers* (the "pink maps") cover the entire country at a scale of 1 1/4 inch per mile. They show footpaths, are impressively accurate, and are now available at chemists and grocery shops, as well as newsagents and bookshops. See Chapter 3, below.

13) *Walking Guidebooks* – These have proliferated in recent years. Their quality can vary widely, but the point is they do exist! The best provide historical and literary background plus notes about geology and wildlife, as well as routefinding directions and sketch maps. Some also provide lists of B&B's and favorite pubs. See Chapter 3, "Maps & Guidebooks."

14) *Human Scale* – An important key to the easy access of the English countryside is its human scale. Vistas are four miles away, not forty, and you can walk there (and back again) in the same afternoon.

Distances in England are about half those in Europe. And the only comparable landscapes in the New World are found in *New* England, and perhaps selected areas of upper New York State.

◊

In summary then – villages are close together, public transport is generally available, most towns and villages have Bed & Breakfast and pubs, guidebooks exist, maps are excellent, the climate is friendly, and the language is recognizably our own. Your pack can weigh as little as 8 to 10 pounds, and you need only comfortable shoes (not boots). A walking trip is also the least expensive way to visit Britain. Walking is a national pastime in England, because it is an *accessible* pastime.

Chapter 2

WALKING BRITAIN, HIKING AMERICA
AND TREKKING EUROPE

HIKING in North America is for the rugged; trekking in Europe is for the rich. Walking in Great Britain is for everyone.

Hiking in America tends to require heavy boots and heavier packs. Distances are large, terrain can be rugged, villages non-existent, food and water scarce, the views magnificent, and the mosquitoes fierce. If you are going for more than a day hike, you need to carry food, shelter and sleeping bag with you.

Trekking in Europe (or anywhere) involves paying a sizable fee for someone else to carry your luggage from place to place, while you amble unencumbered, mingling mostly with others in your tour group. A full meal and warm bed – prearranged – await you at the end of each day. A good outing for those who can afford it, although you socialize mostly with fellow-tourists. Your encounters with local history and local people are usually minimal.

Walking in Britain offers a third alternative. Imagine walking from village to village along waymarked paths through the English countryside, eating at pubs, staying at B&B's (not usually booked ahead), by yourself or with a friend, going at your own pace, spending $35 a day, carrying a pack that weighs eight to ten pounds, wearing shoes not boots, talking with locals who do not treat you like a tourist, exploring Medieval castle ruins in the morning, pausing for lunch beside a Celtic burial mound, feeling the wind in your face as you stride along a 2000-year-old Roman road, walk beneath a Victorian railway viaduct, or follow a green drovers' road through the Yorkshire Dales....

If these things appeal to you, then chances are you will enjoy walking in Britain.

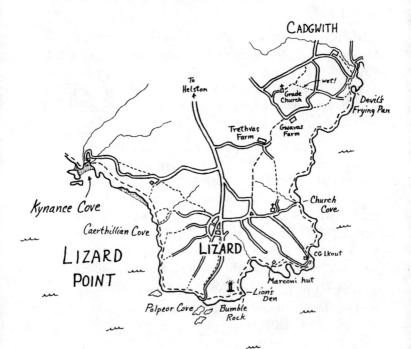

Chapter 3

MAPS AND GUIDEBOOKS

GUIDEBOOKS for walking in Britain abound. Some are useful; others useless; a few invaluable. The best ones are not only accurate with routefinding, but are also good companions along the way – full of humor, history and human stories, with notes about birds, wildflowers, rocks and trees, plus local customs and legends.

Three reasons to buy guidebooks before you go:

- They are hard to find in route – Bookshops make more money from large coffee-table books, nice to look at but of no use as pocket guides.

- They present confusing choices – Many paths have several guides which vary in cost, quality and focus. "Official" guides exist for 15 or so official Long Distance Paths, but are often not the best choice.

  Call travel bookstores. Talk with other walkers. *British Footpath Bibliography: Annotated Guide to Guidebooks* might also help you decide which ones best suit your purpose. (See p. 22, below.)

- They are useful (and fun) to read before your trip – Study the guide before you go to save time and money during your trip. A good guidebook will educate you in a dozen ways about your chosen path or region.

HOW TO TELL A GOOD GUIDEBOOK

A good guidebook is a good companion; a bad one a constant obstruction. Look for the same qualities in a walking guidebook that you look for in a walking companion. For example, they should be reliable and good-humored.

General characteristics to look for:

1. **Sketch Maps**. Can provide details not on other maps – the best route through a farmyard or village, the existence (or absence) of a waymark or footbridge, and so forth.

2. **Detailed, Specific, Clear Route Descriptions**. Beware vagueness, or blanket statements made in an authoritative tone. Avoid the "After you cross the river..." approach, reminiscent of the "After you prepare the vegies..." recipes that take too much for granted. Look for this instead:

> There are two ways to cross the river – by the modern footbridge, and by stepping stones 25 yards upstream. I prefer the stepping stones because they follow the line of a Saxon ford still used in this part of England.

Thus, in two sentences, the writer gives specific directions, a taste of local history, optional routes, and a personal preference based on firsthand experience ... yet leaves us free to choose our own path.

3. **Honesty about Path Difficulties**. A good guide will tell you where the boggy bits are, which landowners are negligent, how slippery a chalk path can be after rain, how piercing the North Wind is even in summer, which villages have no B&B, etc.

4. **Good Humor**. Includes both a sense of humor and a positive tone. The writer should communicate he enjoyed the walk himself. The tone should be sympathetic, not sarcastic. Sarcasm is a sign of those who are weak, in guidebooks as in life. Why waste money and attention on someone else's negative energy?

5. **Literary, Historical, and Geological Notes**. Look for a healthy mix. A good guidebook will make *connections* between these topics and everyday life. The heritage of the past can thus inform the life of the present.

6. **Personal Anecdotes**. Too many can be distracting, but a few good stories convey the author has in fact been there and speaks from firsthand experience. They also communicate the author cares, is emotionally engaged, and is a fellow-traveler who found the journey worthwhile.

7. **Lightweight and Compact**. Other things being equal, go for these. But better a heavy good guidebook than a lightweight bad one.

ORDNANCE SURVEY MAPS

Britain is fortunate in her mapmakers. The Ordnance Survey has made it the best-mapped country in the world.

I. The two series below cover selected tourist areas:

Touring Maps – Brick Red. 1 inch per mile.
   Beautiful topographical maps. Buy these to hang on your wall. Sadly, the scale is slightly too small to be reliably useful to walkers. However, the *back* of each map contains historical notes and tourist tips that are especially well done.

Outdoor Leisure Maps – Yellow. 2 1/2 inches per mile.
   Magnificently detailed and highly priced maps aimed chiefly at tourists. Their detail can feel cluttered at times, however, and their bulk makes them hard to fold in a breeze. Paths are marked with large blunt green dashes.
   This series is also inconveniently divided at times. For example, two *Landranger* maps cover most of the Lake District, whereas four *Outdoor Leisure* maps are required.

II. The following maps cover the entire country:

Landranger Series – Magenta. 1 1/4 inch per mile.

The most useful for most people for most purposes, including walking. Footpaths, pubs, churches, public telephones, youth hostels, burial mounds, and stone circles, etc. are marked on these maps. Paths are marked with small sharp red dashes.

Pathfinder Series – Green. 2 1/2 inches per mile.

Larger scale, but smaller maps. You need more to cover the same area as *Landrangers*. This means they are more costly and more bulky in the end. They are, however, wonderfully clear to follow – less distracting than either Explorer or Outdoor Leisure maps.

Explorer Maps – Orange. 2 1/2 inches per mile.

Intended to replace *Pathfinders* for areas not already covered by Outdoor Leisure maps. These cover more area than Pathfinders, but are quite bulky. Paths are marked with blunt green dashes.

They work best for day walks. Of less value for long distance paths since so many maps are needed.

MAP SUMMARY

Different maps meet different needs, but as a general rule the *Landranger* maps provide the best value:

• They cover more area with no less clarity (at times with greater clarity) than the larger scale maps.

• Paths marked with sharp red dashes tend to be easier to follow than those marked with blunt green dashes.

• A key to good mapmaking is knowing what to leave out. Landrangers excel at this.

• It is significant that *Landrangers* are the maps preferred by the British military.

SOURCES

Maps: In Britain, *Landranger* maps (the "pink maps") are available at local bookshops, newsagents, chemists, and even grocery shops.

In North America you may buy maps from:

- DAVID MORGAN, 11812 Northcreek Pkway N., Suite 103, Bothell WA 98011. Tel 425-485-2132 or 800-324-4934.
- BRITISH TRAVEL SHOP, 551 Fifth Ave, 7th Floor, NY, NY 10019. Tel 212-575-2667 or 800-677-8585.
- BRITISH FOOTPATHS, 914 Mason, Bellingham, WA 98225. Tel 360-671-1217. Queries answered. Catalog available.

◊

Guidebooks: These present special problems because they vary widely in quality and are hard to find in route. Buy and read these *before* you go, whenever possible.

In Britain send your guidebook inquiries to:

- STANFORD'S BOOKS & MAPS, 12/14 Longacre St, London Tel 0171-836-8541. The best selection anywhere.

In North America, sources include:

- UNIVERSITY BOOKSTORE, 4326 University Way, Seattle, WA 98105. Tel 206-634-3400 or 800-335-7323.
- WIDE WORLD BOOKS, 1911-North 45th Street, Seattle, WA 98103. Tel 206-634-3453. Ask for Liz Demsetz.
- GLOBE CORNER BOOKS, 500 Boylston Street, Boston, MA 02116. Tel 617-859-8008. Ask for Pat Carrier.
- TATTERED COVER BOOKS, 1628-16th Street, Denver, CO 80202. Tel 303-322-1965. Selected guidebooks.
- POWELL'S TRAVEL BOOKS, Pioneer Courthouse Square, 701-SW 6th, Portland, OR 97204. Tel 503-228-1108.
- BRITISH FOOTPATHS, 914 Mason, Bellingham, WA 98225. Tel 360-671-1217. Guidebooks & maps. Request Catalog.

UNSCIENTIFIC POSTSCRIPT

A useful resource for those thinking of a walking trip is *British Footpath Bibliography: Annotated Guide to Guidebooks* by R. Hayward (British Footpaths) – which evaluates a broad range of guides and maps for paths and regions throughout England, Wales and Scotland.

This resource (a sort of *Consumer Reports* for walking guides) can help you decide *where* in Britain to go, as well as save you considerable cost in tracking down the right guidebook for your purpose. It:

- discusses pros and cons of different guides and maps.
- includes day walks as well as long distance paths.
- gives sources for maps, guidebooks and B&B lists.

In the end, there is no substitute for testing a guidebook on the path itself, and Hayward's comments offer both the strengths and limits of firsthand experience. Copies may be ordered from your local bookshop, or directly from the publisher (for $10 postpaid). The author invites personal inquiries about particular paths or guides, and offers a full money-back guarantee:

British Footpaths
914 Mason
Bellingham, WA 98225
Tel. 360-671-1217

Chapter 4

MONEY

YOU WILL hear little about walking trips from travel agents. They don't see much profit in this sort of thing. After all, it's hard to spend money on package tours, luxury hotels and gourmet food when you spend your days rambling through the countryside and your evenings talking to locals at the village pub.

Travel agents do profit in the long run from walking trips. First, because you can afford to go back again! Second, because you will *want* to go back since you will feel refreshed, not exhausted, at the end of your trip.

You will of course need a certain amount of money, even on a walking trip – $30 to $40 a day, plus airfare. When you think about it, that's less than most of us need to live at home.

HOW TO CARRY MONEY (1)

I carry it in my wallet and pockets, just as I do at home. Secret money-belts may be a good idea in Marseilles or Naples or Liverpool (although I've never had one in these places either). But pickpockets don't abound in the British countryside. And London, despite rumors to the contrary, remains the safest large city in the western world.

The best defense is an ordinary appearance. If you do not call attention to yourself as a "rich foreign tourist" by your dress or behavior, you need not worry about being mugged. During more than twenty years of traveling in Britain – by train, bus, foot, thumb, plane, taxi and at least one Rolls Royce – I have never been robbed. I have earned money, spent money, lost money and given money away in England. Money has been *returned* to me, but never stolen.

It is possible the legacy of Margaret Thatcher – which widened the gap between rich and poor – may change all this eventually. But it hasn't yet.

HOW TO CARRY MONEY (2)

Traveler's Checks are fine, although you will receive a less favorable exchange rate for your traveler's check dollar than for your cash or Visa dollar.

The best way I have found to obtain money in Britain is to use a Visa DEBIT card for a "cash advance" at one of the four major British banks.

You can avoid Visa fees by using a debit card rather than a conventional credit card. Debit cards are available from brokerage companies such as CHARLES SCHWAB *at no cost*, as well as from some commercial banks.

The procedure is as follows:

- Acquire a Visa or MasterCard debit card.
  (American Express and Discover cards will not work for cash advances at banks. Sorry.)

- Take your debit card into any branch of Midland, Lloyds, Barclays, or National Westminster Bank.
  (Most villages have at least one branch bank.)

- Request a "cash advance" from any ordinary teller.
  (No need to wait in line for the International Teller.)

Two minutes and one brief phone call later, you have your money and are on your way. No hassle, no delay. Unlike with traveler's checks, there is *no bank fee* from the English bank. You receive the exchange rate that obtains when your transaction reaches your bank back home, which can be a few days or weeks later. Currency markets are then searched electronically for the best rate.

◊

You can get £100 or so at the airport upon your arrival. Then use your debit card to replenish cash during the trip. Think in terms of about £25 a day for walking days.

You can also get British pounds before you go from any major American bank. But this will cost more than using a foreign exchange booth upon your arrival.

Using an airport kiosk such as Thomas Cook is highly convenient and less pricey than it seems, since using a debit card means you get the optimal exchange rate above (*not* the one posted at the kiosk).

There is a small transaction fee, but this usually is less than postage your bank charges to transfer foreign currency to your local branch, and you also receive a better exchange rate than your local bank is able to offer.

◊

Automatic Teller Machines are increasingly common and work with cards such as *Cirrus,* but ATM's are harder to find in the countryside than branch banks.

Exchange rates are generally better in England or any host country when buying foreign currency with US dollars, because the dollar is (generally) a desirable currency to own on the international market.

SAMPLE BUDGET

£13-18	B&B per person. Will vary widely. (Youth hostels would be about £5 less.)
1	Apple, Kendal Mint Cake, or your favorite bikkies as nibble food.
3	Half-pint and sandwich for lunch at a pub. (optional)
6	Hot evening meal at a pub or restaurant. (Fish & Chips even cheaper.)
2	Special Purchase (Souvenir or admission fee or local guidebook or extra map; OR Save toward a wool sweater at the end of your trip, etc.)

£20-25	Without lunch or special purchase. (@ $1.65 = $33-42 / day per person)
£25-30	With lunch and special purchase. (@ $1.65 = $42-50 / day per person)†

$33/day + $600* air fare = 2 weeks for $1100.
1 month for $1600.

$50/day + $600* air fare = 2 weeks for $1300.
1 month for $2100.

† For time spent in or near London, double your cost per day. Budget also does not include train or bus travel within Britain. Allow £60 round trip ($95) for travel from London to the Lake District, Yorkshire, Cornwall, or Wales.

* For tips on low airfares, please see Chapter 9.

Chapter 5

ENGLISH FOOD

AMERICAN travelers, it seems, complain more often and more loudly about food than about anything else! So let me warn you ahead of time....

Do not go to England for gourmet delights and high cuisine. If you want fancy food, go to France or Italy, where they care intensely about food. In England they care about other things – like the countryside and comfortable shoes, or the Lifeboat Society and English beer. Gourmet cooking you find in England is likely to be by foreigners who have opened restaurants for the tourist trade.

Howsoeverbeit, here are some foods I have survived on while walking in Britain. Chances are, you won't starve either:

English Breakfast – Egg, bacon, sausage, stewed tomato, fruit juice, cereal, toast and jam, tea or coffee. Sometimes also mushrooms, potatoes, baked beans, or fruit salad.... This is why you don't need to eat again until dinner! If you don't care for fried eggs, most B&B hosts will be happy to scramble, poach or boil them for you. Ask politely.

Fresh Fruits (and Vegies) – Found at most grocery shops. My favorites are small Granny Smith apples.

Fish & Chips – Fingerfood wrapped in paper, with salt and malt vinegar. Still the least expensive full meal. Done properly, the chips are surprisingly non-greasy.

English Tea – Served very strong, with milk and sugar. Goes well with English rain.

English Beer – Food in itself. The difference between American beer (lagers) and English beer (bitters, ales and stouts) is the difference between Wonderbread and 12-Grain-Whole-Kernel-Wheat-&-Honey Special.

Experiment with different local brews. English beer is a subject dear to the English heart. Which ones you love (or hate), will prove tantalizing and spirited conversation with the locals.

English Sweets – You're going to have fun with these. Try Bounty Bars and Kendal Mint Cakes among candies; Bourbon Creams and Club Biscuits among bikkies (cookies). My special favorites, however, are McVitties Plain Chocolate Homewheat Biscuits. Ahh....

Pastries – English bakery shops are usually worth a visit. Try sausage rolls (savory) and Eccles cakes (sweet).

Cheese – From Cheshire to Swaledale, local regions often have their own. And kings have killed for the recipes (e.g., Wensleydale Cheese). After you've had the local cheese, try the local ice cream!

Pub Grub – Good value and increasingly common. No longer just meat pies and ploughman's lunches. Pubs now serve a variety of full meals, from lasagne and curries, to vegetarian dishes and specialty soups. An evening meal will typically be served from 7 to 9 PM.

Asian Food – Indian and Pakistani restaurants fill the role of Chinese restaurants in America, providing a taste of the exotic without exotic cost. Try the different curries. Chinese food, while also good, is not cheap.

Chapter 6

PUBS

THE NEW WORLD has nothing comparable to the two English institutions of Pubs and Bed & Breakfast.

Pubs first: Virtually every town or village has at least one, and they are marked on Ordnance Survey maps as *PH* or *Inn*. About three-fourths of Britain's pubs are owned by a local brewery; about one-fourth are "free houses" able to sell beer from any brewery they choose. Recent legal changes favor free houses, and work against the tendency of large breweries to dominate the market.

Neighborhood pubs function as community centers. People go not so much to drink as to be with friends, share local gossip, and play pub games such as darts, dominoes, skittles, and shove-ha'penny. A typical pub will have a Lounge Bar (for meals), a Public Bar (for darts), and a Back Garden (with flowers, play area for kids, plus tables for eating).

Many pubs now serve good food at reasonable prices. Pubs have stepped in to fill the niche between fast food and posh restaurants, to provide home-cooked meals at prices ordinary people can afford. They have done this to regain market share since England joined the Common Market and local beer sales came under pressure from European wine merchants.

One result is that pubs now attract more families than ever before. Discrimination against women has greatly diminished. "Children Welcome" signs are springing up. Family Rooms are becoming common. And pub gardens often have slides and swings for kids to play on while their parents have a quiet drink.

Hours of opening are no longer restricted by law. These will vary from village to village, and pub to pub. A useful rule of thumb is from 11 AM to 3 PM, and from 6 to 11 PM. An evening meal is typically served from 7 to 9 PM.

Non-alcoholic drinks such as soft drinks, fruit juices and coffee (but not tea!) are routinely available. I have seen Diet Pepsi on tap next to the local ale.

Tipping is not customary at English pubs – another way you will save money by eating at the local pub.

◊

Apart from tourist pubs – usually attached to luxury hotels or advertised as Wine Bars – English pubs tend to be informal places full of homey touches and friendly people. Many are centuries old, and some were originally private houses. Others offer accommodation, much as did earlier coaching inns and drovers' inns.

Few experiences can match the sense of welcome that comes from spending an hour in a good English pub. Pubs are not intimidating, but inviting and cosy. And being cosy, they are at the very heart of English life!

Chapter 7

BED AND BREAKFAST

EXPERIENCING the unique personal touches of a village Bed & Breakfast is an important part of the human dimension of walking in England.

The term "B&B" has become fashionable in America, but the New World has nothing quite like a traditional English Bed and Breakfast. Ours are more regulated, more formal and more expensive.

Guest and *Host* defines the fundamental relationship. For most Bed & Breakfast hosts, making money is not their primary motive, and having everything your own way should not be yours. Thus, expect some time limitation on breakfast (usually between 8 and 9 AM). Also, don't expect a private bathroom. The toilet and bath or shower will usually be down the hall, and shared with other guests or family members. You may have to wait in line for your bath ... just like at home.

Accommodation, simple to elaborate, ranges from:

- **B&B** – Private house with 1 or 2 spare rooms.
- **Guest House** – Ditto, with 4 or 5 rooms. Slightly more structured and slightly more expensive.
- **Pubs/Small Hotels or Inns** – Still quite informal. Costs a little more but still good value.

- **Farmhouse B&B** – Prices vary, but a good farmhouse B&B is hard to beat, with larger rooms and more food than usual.
- **Luxury Hotels** – Same as elsewhere in the world.

HOW TO FIND BED & BREAKFAST

Accommodation guides exist for many paths, and can be worth their weight in gold. *British Footpath Bibliography,* (British Footpaths), explains where to get these.

Stilwell's *National Trail Companion* provides brief, but well-chosen B&B lists for over forty long distance paths. The Ramblers Association (1/5 Wandsworth Road, London) publishes a more eclectic but still useful countrywide list of B&B's that cater for walkers.

These B&B lists will help you plan your trip, and are comforting to have with you in route. Since the best B&B's are impromptu discoveries, however, let me suggest the following approach which also works well:

1) **Arrive early** – perhaps 4 to 5 PM (before the car traffic) – and shop around for yourself. Do this, and you'll almost never need to book ahead, even in high summer.

2) **Look for Signs**. Choose a street or neighborhood, and look around for B&B signs hanging outside the front door or beside the front gate. If there are several, pick the house and garden that attracts you most, knock on the door, and ask to be shown a room.

3) **Ask a Local**. If there are no obvious B&B signs (or you are too tired to look for them), then find someone who looks local and ask if he or she knows anyone who does B&B. I have found locals in grocery shops, in laundrettes, or most often simply walking along the street. Don't be shy; people will not consider you odd for asking.

4) **Pubs, Chemists, Bakeries**. Pubkeepers and pharmacists are infinite sources of local knowledge. Bakeries are other good places to ask. In Wales, go to the Post Office and ask for a Welsh-speaking B&B, where they will charge you less and feed you more (plus teach you a few Welsh words).

5) **Tourist Information Center (TIC)**. If you cannot find signs or locals (or you are feeling lazy), then go to the TIC where for a small fee they will arrange lodging for you. The disadvantage is that you don't get to see the room, sit down on the bed, or meet the host first. The advantage is that you save time and effort.

When closed, most TIC's post a list of local accommodation on their door, which gives names, addresses, phone numbers and prices. A valuable list. Use it.

6) **Police Station**. In any town or village the police will have an Accommodation List that is even more complete than the Tourist Information Center's list. Again, the police will not consider you a nuisance, but will be friendly and helpful.

7) **Recommendations from other Bed and Breakfasts**. Don't hesitate to inquire at houses with "No Vacancy" signs. A remarkable network exists among Bed & Breakfast hosts, and some of the best B&B's result from personal recommendations.

WHAT TO EXPECT

- A friendly host, and some personal interaction (advice, directions, where you went that day, what their favorite local walks or shops are, help with small personal matters, etc.). They are after all letting you into their home, and are as interested in establishing some feeling of personal trust and rapport as you are.

- A smallish but cosy room, with homey touches such as flowers, books, wallpaper, or homemade quilt.

- A decent bed. *Decent* does not mean Sealy Posturepedic! But it does mean you can expect more than a deep valley mattress. If not satisfied, simply explain you have a bad back and no feelings are hurt.

- To be shown the room before deciding. If the host does not volunteer, it is OK to ask "May I please see the room?" But remember your role as *guest*, and ask politely. Don't demand.

- No extra charge for bath or shower. Sometimes there will only be one of these, not both.

- No extra charge for a full English breakfast.

- A washbasin in your room, but no private bath or toilet. These will be down the hall, shared with other guests. Sometimes *en suite* rooms with a private bathroom will be available for an extra charge.

  (Note: En suite rooms generally have only a shower, whereas a hot *bath* – shared or otherwise – can be a delicious luxury at the end of a long walking day.)

- Soap and Towel provided, although not a "face cloth." Carry your own wash cloth.

- Breakfast sometime between 8 and 9 AM. 8:30 is typical.

– Check-out time from 10 to 10:30 on the morning of your departure. Often you can leave your luggage (neatly packed) for all or part of the day if you are catching an afternoon train or bus, and want to be unencumbered to sightsee during the day.

UNEXPECTED TOUCHES

– A public lounge or sitting room with TV, books, etc. Fairly common, but I would still count it as an extra. Sometimes this will be shared with the host family, sometimes not.

– Coffee and/or Tea-making facilities in your room. Likewise fairly common, but consider it an extra.

– Host welcomes you with tea and bikkies (cookies) when you arrive in the afternoon.

– Morning tea delivered to your room *before* breakfast. Can be a startling experience if you aren't prepared!

– A Hot Water bottle in your bed. (Sometimes happens if your B&B does not have central heating.)

– To be adopted by the family dog or cat.

– To sit down with the host family at the breakfast table. (Rare, but it does happen.)

LONDON

Finally, none of the above applies to London!

Well, very seldom.... Affordable, friendly lodgings can still be found in London – in neighborhoods such as Paddington, Euston, and Bloomsbury. But the big city is still no match for the countryside when it comes to the personal touch. Little amenities, such as a public lounge or tea-making facilities in your room, are less common. Your host will often be a hired manager rather than a resident owner. Even a full English breakfast cannot be assumed. And for these diminished services you can expect to pay from two to three times what you would pay in a town or village.

If these things do not appeal, remember that's one reason you chose a walking trip rather than a tourist trek.

Chapter 8

YOUTH HOSTELS

ENGLAND AND WALES have some of the best youth hostels in the world. (Scotland claims the *very* best.) There are some 240 hostels scattered about England and Wales. A few are purpose-built; others are former manor houses, hunting lodges, gothic mansions, Georgian watermills and Victorian cottages ... plus at least one old golf clubhouse. (No history buff will find Britain's youth hostels dull.)

All offer convenience, cleanliness, hot showers, drying rooms for wet clothing, friendly wardens, and low cost. Many also serve homecooked meals – sometimes with a greater menu selection than B&Bs or pubs.

Youth hostels are an excellent way to encounter fellow travelers eager to swap stories and share meals. There is no age limit; "youth" refers to anyone young enough in spirit to welcome adventure and make new friends. Apart from school parties, the average age is perhaps forty.

◊

To stay at a hostel you will need to join the Youth Hostel Association (YHA) for a modest annual fee of £10 or so. You do not have to join before you leave home. You can join on the spot. If you stay two nights at youth hostels during your trip, you break even with B&B prices.

Youth hostels typically cost £7 to £10, plus optional breakfast (£3) and supper (£5). They also offer packed lunches (£3) – which are good value, and can be saved for supper the next evening if there is no convenient pub.

Hostels also provide a fully equipped kitchen for those who prefer to cook their own food. Please leave it clean and tidy for the next person.

◊

The rooms are usually dormitory style, with bunk beds. If the hostel is not full, the warden may spread people out so you sometimes get a room to yourself. Lights out will be at 11 or 11:30 PM.

Blankets, pillows, and bed linens are furnished. Soap and towels are not furnished, but in practice can usually be arranged, sometimes for a small extra charge. Ask politely. (You could also carry a small towel and soap as emergency back-ups, but these are rarely needed.)

The front desk usually sells selected food items such as tinned soup, fruit, biscuits (cookies), sweets (candies) and other nonperishables. Sometimes the hostel also sells maps and guidebooks for the local area.

◊

Rooms are segregated by sexes – with a men's wing and a women's wing. In practice, the rules are fairly flexible. If the hostel is not too full, the warden is sometimes able to give couples and families a private room, especially if you ask in advance. Again, ask politely.

Most hostels are open from 7 to 10 AM, and 5 to 11 PM. Some are open longer, but wardens have other lives too. It is a good idea to ring ahead (before 10 AM or after 5 PM) to reserve a place. The warden can also "book-a-bed-ahead" for you at another hostel.

◊

You may of course prefer traditional Bed & Breakfast when given a choice. I admit I generally do. Yet Britain's youth hostels (like Britain's pubs) are too rich an experience to banish from your travel map altogether.

It would be sad for anyone to avoid youth hostels simply because they were unfamiliar or vaguely intimidating. (All those kids, all those health nuts, all those *serious* hikers, all those strange accents, all those people! ... or whatever.)

Occasionally a youth hostel will in fact be the *best* place to stay in a given area – such as Pwll Deri along the Pembrokeshire coast, or Keld in Swaledale. At such times it will feel good to whisk out the youth hostel arrow from your quiver of possibilities, and – effortlessly – score another British bullseye.

◊

At Bed & Breakfasts you will meet more *locals* (including the hosts). At youth hostels, you will meet more *travelers*, and especially fellow walkers.

A youth hostel (including breakfast) will cost roughly £5 less than B&B. You could thus reduce daily expenses to as low as £15 ($25) – while still enjoying the amenities of hot shower, warm bed, good food, and friendly people.

Youth hostels thus become yet another way the English countryside is *accessible* to ordinary people.

Chapter 9

WHAT TO DO BEFORE YOU GO

1. **Buy and read guidebook for your proposed walk.**

   This will save time, hassle and money during your trip. A good guidebook will provide literary, historical and geological background, as well as tell you which stile to cross over.

   Where to find guidebooks, and how to choose the best one for your purpose, are topics unto themselves. Please see Chapter 3, "Maps and Guidebooks."

2. **Acquire an Accommodation Guide for your walk.**

   B&B lists exist for long distance paths (LDP's), and can be quite useful. *British Footpath Bibliography,* by R. Hayward (British Footpaths), explains where to get these for specific paths.*

   The best general source is Stillwell's *National Trail Companion,* which has B&B lists for over 40 LDP's, and is available from some travel bookstores for about $20. You can then copy relevant pages to take with you.

   ---

   *British Footpaths also provides B&B lists free with all guidebook purchases.

3. **Buy and study Landranger Maps for your walk.**

Consider marking maps ahead of time with a yellow Hi-liter pen. In Britain the maps are readily available at local shops. In America you may buy them from:

DAVID MORGAN, 11812 Northcreek Pkwy N, Suite 103, Bothell WA 98011. Tel 425-485-2132. Request catalog.

BRITISH TRAVEL SHOP, 551 Fifth Ave, 7th Floor, NY, NY 10019. Tel 212-490-6688. Request Catalog.

BRITISH FOOTPATHS, 914 Mason, Bellingham WA 98225 Tel 360-671-1217. Request Catalog. Queries answered.

4. **Test your pack.**

Fill your rucksack and go for a two-mile walk in your favorite park. If your pack doesn't feel comfortable, adjust or lighten the load until it does. A little trouble now will save a lot of misery later.

(See Chapter 9, "Packing Light.")

5. **Test your shoes.**

Especially if they are new, be sure to test them for comfort, sturdiness, and water resistance.

(See Chapter 9, "Packing Light.")

6. **Use more than one Travel Agent.**

Airfares are too complicated for any one agent to know them all. Ask several for the lowest fare. You might also try *Travel Professionals*, Seattle WA – (206) 236-0990, or (800) 523-8559. A sign on their front door reads LOWEST FARE GUARANTEED! I have found them to be good as their word. Ask for Bobbie Sundsten (who is British) or Rob Austin.

7. Avoid Sunday arrivals if possible.

Train and bus schedules are curtailed on Sundays, and many shops and Tourist Information Centers are closed. Saturday train and bus services are usually quite good.

8. Avoid arriving on a Bank Holiday Weekend.

The British take their public holidays seriously, and head for the seaside or the mountains. Your trip will be off to a better start if you don't begin it when everyone else is also beginning theirs.

The eight Bank Holidays are worth learning:

2   Christmas & Boxing Day (day after Christmas).

1   New Year's Day.

2   Easter (Good Friday and Easter Monday).

1   May Bank Holiday: first Monday in May.
      Corresponds to European Labor Day.

1   Spring Bank Holiday: last Monday in May.
      Corresponds to American Memorial Day.

1   August Bank Holiday: last Monday in August.
      Corresponds to American Labor Day.

9. Acquire a Visa or MasterCard debit card.

From your local bank, or from Charles Schwab (free). Using a debit card for a cash advance at a British bank is the easiest way (any branch, any teller) and cheapest way (best rate, no bank fee) to obtain money while in rural Britain. Only *Visa* and *MasterCard* have arrangements with British banks for no-fee cash advances.

(See Chapter 4, "Money.")

10. **Buy £100 to £200 to take with you.** (optional)
    You may purchase British pounds through any major US bank. It can, however, be both troublesome and expensive to do this before you leave. Much simpler – and usually cheaper – is to use an airport kiosk upon your arrival.

    (See Chapter 10, "Day of Arrival.")

11. **Consider reading *The National Trust Book of Long Walks*,** by Adam Nicolson (Pan/Crown). This is the liveliest general book about Long Distance Paths in Britain. Nicolson describes the physical and historical features of a dozen different routes with the relish and detail of firsthand experience. Exceptional photographs will whet your appetite still further. Available through U.S. bookshops.

    British Footpath Sampler, by Richard Hayward (British Footpaths), is especially useful for those who consider themselves "walkers" rather than "hikers."

12. **Consider joining the Ramblers Association.**
    1/5 Wandsworth Road, London, England SW8 2XX (Tel 01144-171-582-6878). The RA has a quarterly magazine and a *Rambler's Yearbook & Accommodation Guide,* which gives a countrywide list of B&B's that cater for walkers. I sometimes use it as a supplement to the B&B lists for individual paths, mentioned in #2 above.

    The *Rambler's Yearbook* may also be purchased from British bookshops, or directly from the RA by non-members for about £10.

13. **Take a look at general travel guides.**

• *Michelin, Baedecker, Automobile Association (AA),* and *Shell* guides are excellent, but too detailed for most purposes.

• *Fodor's* and *Fielding's* guides are not so good; these tend to be dull and impersonal.

• Arthur Frommer's *Dollarwise Guides* are perhaps the best value for most people. They are clearly written, with no-nonsense advice on prices and excellent brief histories of cities and regions.

• *Let's Go Britain* is also good, but with a youthful bias toward what is trendy. Not surprising, since written by Harvard students.

Chapter 10

PACKING LIGHT: 10 POUNDS OR LESS

PREPARATION

Physical and mental preparation are relatively easy. The emotional preparation is the hard part.

- **Physical** – Put on your pack and take a walk in your favorite park. Then window-shop for an hour. If your pack is uncomfortable or too heavy, keep adjusting or repacking until it works. If you can't get it to work, find another pack.

- **Mental** – Review the guide for your proposed walk. A good guidebook will give not only routefinding details but also historical and geological background. See Appendices for a few recommended guidebooks.

- **Emotional** – Convincing yourself you don't need the kitchen sink to survive a few weeks away from home – that's the tricky bit!

PACK

If your full pack weighs ten pounds or less, then design is not critical. Contour-fit, wide hip belt, or even padded shoulder straps are not essential, so long as the pack itself feels comfortable to you.

Most hikers in America use either a small daypack, or a large backpack to carry tent and sleeping bag. Neither size suits your purpose. You will want a "mid-size pack" (1800 to 2400 cubic inches).

Mid-size packs are not common in American camping stores. Therefore expect some shopping around, a few incredulous looks, and don't be too surprised if you have to special-order a pack.

Packs I can recommend:

KELTY	*M-G Convertible*	(1-800-423-2320)
KELTY	*Wyndham*	(1-800-423-2320)
JANSPORT	*Super Sack*	(1-800-558-3600)

The first Kelty "converts" into a belt-bag for use as a day pack. Its capacity is about 1800 cubic inches, and I have used mine happily for the past fifteen years, once staying as long as two months. The other two packs do not convert to day packs, but have more compartments and padded shoulder straps.*

Any camping store should be able to special order these or similar mid-size packs for you. In Seattle *The Swallow's Nest* (2308-6th Ave., Seattle WA 98138, Tel 206-441-4100) carries the Kelty packs. So does *Base Camp* in Bellingham, Washington (Tel 360-733-5461).

◊

The 800 numbers above may also be used to contact the manufacturers directly, to ask about their latest mid-size packs, or to learn the names of local dealers near you.

---

*Padded shoulder straps can be added to the first Kelty quite easily with some bits of corduroy, foam, and velcro.

SHOES

The spectrum ranges from leather hiking boots (heavy), to lightweight Gortex boots (expensive), to running shoes (porous). Soft leather shoes that can be oiled also work. In the end COMFORT is the only essential, and no one else can decide for you.

Three general comments:

• Shoes that breathe will be more comfortable than those that don't.

• Slightly oversize shoes will allow room for wool socks. When you are not wearing thick socks, the extra room can be filled with removable insoles.

• Over stony terrain (such as in the Lake District) lightweight boots or shoes with sturdy soles will be more comfortable to the soles of your feet.

My current favorites are CLARKS *Natureveldts* and ECCO *TrackII/Gore-Tex* walking shoes. I have found these to be both comfortable and waterproof. Most camping stores and serious shoe shops, such as Nordstroms, can order them for you. Don't forget to check discount shoe stores such as Shoe Pavilion, which often carry name brands at half the cost of specialty shoe shops.

◊

Women's shoes present major frustrations. A curious conspiracy seems to separate style and fashion from comfort and sturdiness. If you already own running shoes or walking shoes, remember the best shoes for mall walking are not necessarily the best shoes for footpath walking. CLARKS makes two sturdy walking shoes for women (*Smooth Walker* and *Air Walker*), although I have not tested either of these personally. ECCO, EASY SPIRIT and

ROCKPORT all make leather "walking shoes" for women. Once again, no one else can tell you what feels comfortable to *your* feet.

◊

Lightweight boots, for men or for women, are somewhat easier to find. Although I'm not a boots person myself, those made by BRASHER (British), RAICHLÉ (Swiss), ECCO (Danish), and ZAMBERLAN (Italian) are among the best, and will cost less if bought in Britain.

◊

Finally, if you have special problems finding shoes that fit your feet, I can also recommend:

SARA'S SHOES
5638 County Road 102
Guffey, Colorado 80820

Sara McIntosh is an enterprising Scotswoman and a full-fledged cobbler, who will make a pair of walking shoes for you for about the same cost as a pair of *Rocksports*. They are not as superficially elegant as commercial shoes, or as water-resistant as CLARKS *Natureveldts*. But they are comfortable. I walked ten miles the first day in mine, and my feet didn't hurt....

I was impressed. You will be, too.

WEATHERGEAR

When you go on a walking trip in Britain, expect to get rained on from time to time. Don't worry, you won't melt or drown. And you should understand nothing will keep you perfectly dry in a driving rain in Cornwall or the Lake District. People have different tolerances for getting wet, so it is finally a matter of personal preference. Some will want to add rain pants to their gear. Others will take only a thin windbreaker to wear over their wool sweater.

The five essential items are:

- **Rain Jacket.** This ranges from a true impermeable (keeps the wet out but the sweat in) to a Gortex jacket (works in all but driving rain, costly and fairly bulky) to a nylon windbreaker (compact and lightweight, lets the rain in after five minutes, but also dries in five minutes after the rain stops).

- **Hat/Cap with a brim.** For sun and snow as well as rain. I have worn mine more as a sun hat than as a rain hat. I use a little white roll-up hat which doubles as a fisherman's hat or a cricketeer's cap, depending on the social context.

- **Thin Mittens.** Wool or Polypropylene. With *mittens* (vs gloves) your fingers can keep each other warm.

- **Thin Wool Sweater.** Wool keeps you warm even when wet. Lambswool and Marino (Botany) wool are thinner and less bulky than (but just as warm as) Shetland and Icelandic wool.

- **Wool Socks.** At least one pair. Will keep your feet warm even when wet. The best ones have a loop-pile knit on the inside for extra cushioning. Your wool socks can also double as slippers, for padding down the hallway to the loo in the middle of the night.

PACKING LIST

Generic packing lists are a dime a dozen. Here is an actual packing list that has worked for a real person.... I've used it, with minor changes, for many years. This will not be your packing list in every detail. But I invite you to use it as a springboard to create your own. Small 1 and 2 ounce plastic bottles are available at any camping store.

CLOTHING

1 long pants + belt
1 walking shorts
1 short sleeve shirt
1 white T-shirt
2 pattern T-shirts
Thin wool sweater
3 or 4 underpants
2 pair lightweight socks
1 pair wool socks
1 pair shoes
Lightweight rain jacket
Hat or cap
Thin mittens

In pockets:
  wallet, knife
  pen, memo book,
  comb

Women add:
  lightwt nightie,
  bra, scarf,
  make-up kit,
  band for hair

TOILET ARTICLES (*Everyday use*)

Shampoo (2 oz.)
Lotion (2 oz.)
Toothpaste (2 oz.)
Toothbrush (folding)
Wash cloth + plastic bag

Dental floss
Disposable razors
Deodorant (1/2 oz.)
Aftershave (1/2 oz.)

HOUSEHOLD (*Occasional use*)

Mink oil (2 oz.)
Nail clippers
Rolaids
Anacin tin
Vitamin C (500 mg/1 oz.)

Kleenex
Chapstick
Sunscreen (1 oz.)
Plastic spoon
Foam heel pads

FIRST AID (*Emergency use*)

Band Aids
Antiseptic (1/2 oz. tube)
Small Ace bandage
Ben Gay (small tube)
Small gauze pad
First aid tape
Tweezers
"Second Skin" or Moleskin

Eyedrops for dust
Needle and thread
Small bar of soap
Extra pocket comb
Extra shoelaces
Extra camera battery
Extra eyeglass screws

PORTABLE OFFICE / PURSE

Envelopes for air tickets, passport, Visa, receipts, extra £, etc.
Journal pages or memo book
Extra pen
Address list
Hi-liter pen to mark map
Compass

MISCELLANEOUS

Guidebook and Maps (in waterproof plastic bag)
Nylon food bag (with carrying straps)
Plastic water bottle
Camera + pouch
Film (in ziplock bag)
Extra ziplock bag

◊

I keep **First Aid, Toilet Articles, Household Items,** and my **Portable Office** in four separate nylon pouches.

◊

I line the main compartment of my pack with a sturdy plastic bag, into which I place my clothing. No pack will keep its contents completely dry in a driving rain, so why not be prepared? This seems like ridiculous overkill on a sunny day, but when the rains do come I can relax.

A small word of caution: Don't go home, spread these items out on your bed, and complain they weigh more than ten pounds. Remember, you will be wearing half your clothes, plus carrying your water bottle and camera on your belt.

What about dress clothes and an extra pair of shoes for London theater and concerts? If you want these feel free, but you will not need them. The British are more relaxed about surface formalities than Americans. They are more used to thinking of the arts as part of everyday life. At any typical concert or play you will see both jeans and tuxedos. Neither will seem out of place. Suit yourself is the best rule of thumb.

The only time you will *need* a suit is at a royal wedding, or at one of those (rare) snooty pubs that uses a dress code to keep the tourists out during lunch.

IF YOU TAKE TOO MUCH

If you bring more than you need (and I still do, despite my best efforts), you have several options:

1. **Use Left Luggage.**

   Main line railway stations have *Left Luggage* rooms that are open long hours, and have attendants. It is well worth paying a few extra pounds to save carrying a few extra pounds.

   This is also an easy way to store a city wardrobe (should you want one), until you return to London at the end of your trip.

   You can also check items at Heathrow and Gatwick airports. I try to avoid these and Victoria Rail Station, however, since the cost of Left Luggage is higher at these heavily touristed places.

2. Mail items ahead to yourself.

Send them c/o *Poste Restante* (= General Delivery). For example, if you plan to visit York during your trip, you can post books, maps and clothing you won't need until then to yourself c/o the York Post Office.

Address the package to:

YOURSELF
Poste Restante
York
North Yorkshire

3. Mail items back to the U.S.A.

This will be significantly cheaper if you use *Surface* Mail rather than Air Mail. Expect packages to take from 6 to 8 weeks to arrive.

- Books and maps may be sent book rate. The magic words to write on your parcel are <u>Printed Papers, Surface</u>. Maximum weight per pkg is five kilograms (11 pounds).

- Other items (clothing, gifts, etc.) may be sent by <u>Small Packet, Surface</u> rate if they weigh less than one kilo. (2.2 pounds).

Your parcels should be "unsealed" to make them easy to open for customs inspection. Therefore, do not seal them with tape or tightly knotted string. Best to use a "Jiffy Bag" (padded manila envelope) with special clips that make it simple to open and reclose. Loosely knotted string may also be used. You can buy jiffy bags at the post office, or at newsagents, bookshops, and stationers shops.

Finally, you need to fill out a small green customs declaration, which will be taped to your package (e.g., "books and maps worth approx. $25").

LAUNDRY

Laundromats are fairly common in Britain, and are called "laundrettes." They are frequently staffed and you can then simply leave your clothes and return for them later. Laundrettes still require extra time and timing, however, so I prefer a different approach.

I wash my socks, shirt and underwear every night in the bathroom at my B&B. I then *wring these out in a dry towel*, and they are dry by morning. Shirts that are 65/35% cotton/poly still breathe well enough to be comfortable, but keep their shape better and dry faster than 100% cotton shirts.

For soaked shoes and other minor emergencies, don't hesitate to ask your Bed & Breakfast host for help. Use courtesy and common sense, however. Wet shoes are one thing; *mucky* shoes are another. You would not want someone tracking mud into your house, so don't track mud into theirs.

Chapter 11

DAY OF ARRIVAL

• **Consider saving London for the end of your trip.**

You'll enjoy it more and spend less. You won't be jetlagged, plus you will "know the ropes" better, and feel more comfortable in a foreign country near the end of your trip than at the beginning.

• **Get £100 cash advance at the airport. (optional)**

Use a debit card at a foreign exchange kiosk (such as Thomas Cook) to buy a few British pounds as starter cash. Use branch banks for larger sums later, since banks charge *no fee* for cash advances.

If you use your debit card for British Rail tickets and special purchases, you can save your cash for daily expenses. Expect to spend about £25 per person on walking days.

• **Buy a train ticket to your destination at the airport.**

At Gatwick Airport, go to the *British Rail Travel Centre*. At Heathrow Airport, go to the *British Rail Travel Desk*. The BR Travel Desk at Heathrow moves around, so ask an airport employee for directions when you arrive.

I use my Visa card to pay for this ticket, and keep cash for smaller daily expenses. Expect to pay about £60 ($95) for a *return* (round trip ticket) to Yorkshire, the Lake District, Wales, or Cornwall.

- **Buy a Return (round trip) vs a Single (one way) ticket.**
  A return often costs only a few dollars more, and is usually worth getting as cheap insurance, even if at the time you do not plan to use it. Plans can change.

- **Travel time by train to your destination is typically between 2 and 4 hours.** If your flight arrives by mid-afternoon you will reach your destination before dark, and in time to book B&B on your arrival. Daylight lasts until 9 or 10 PM during spring and summer.

- **Heathrow Airport offers several travel options.**
  Heathrow to Victoria Rail Station (central London) via London Underground (Tube) takes about 45 minutes. At Victoria switch to the tube line that will take you to the rail station your train is scheduled to leave from – such as Euston, Kings Cross, or Waterloo.

  From Heathrow, frequent buses connect to BritRail at *Reading* and *Woking*, for points west and south.

  Express Rail Service from Heathrow to Paddington – new in summer 1998 – takes only 20 minutes to reach Paddington Railway Station.

- **Frequent trains link Gatwick Airport to Victoria Rail Station in central London.**
  Travel time is about 30 minutes. The green buses from the airport to London cost less, but take much longer. Once at Victoria, follow the same procedure as above.

  You can often catch a train *directly* to your destination from Gatwick, if you are headed south or west.

- **Bed and Breakfast for your first night.**
  Does not usually have to be booked ahead. If you wish to book ahead, consider phoning rather than writing. A 3-minute call costs less than $3 if you direct-dial.

Pick a B&B from one of the Accommodation Guides mentioned in Chapter 9. Dial *011 + Country Code + City Code + Number*. If unsure of area codes, dial the International Operator (00) and ask. For example:

011-44-171-836-8541 is Stanford's Books & Maps.

011-44-171-582-6878 is the Ramblers Association.

Finally, note the time difference – 8 hours on the west coast, 5 hours on the east coast. Thus, 5 PM in Britain will be 9 AM of the same day in Seattle or San Francisco, and 12 noon in New York or Atlanta.

• Jet Lag.

Cannot be avoided. Best antidotes are to *walk* and *eat!* Take a twenty-minute walk and breathe fresh air. Eat when it is mealtime at your destination, regardless of when you ate last.

Jet lag can be diminished somewhat by not drinking alcohol during the flight and by closing your eyes for at least three hours during the trip. If you can sleep, all the better. But *rest with eyes closed* is almost as effective.

Go to bed early, and expect to wake up early the first morning. Relax, and go with the flow.

• Left Luggage.

If you do bring extra baggage, use the Left Luggage service provided at all main-line railway stations. Again, it's worth paying a few extra pounds to avoid carrying a few extra pounds.

If you begin your trip in London – even if only to change trains – you can use the opportunity to leave excess gear, which you will not need until you return to London at the end of your trip.

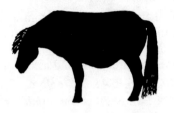

Chapter 12

PACE

TIME AND DISTANCE can be tricky dimensions when traveling. Your personal sense of time speeds up, while real-world time seems to slow down. The present flashes by with incredible fullness, yet when you consult the calendar, what *felt* like a long month will turn out to have been a short week.

This is especially true when you are rambling through the English countryside. The sheer density of experience – the people, the history, the natural beauty – can be almost overwhelming. I have walked all day, met enough people and encountered enough history to last a short lifetime, yet at the end of the day found that I had only walked three miles!

This will happen to you too…. It's OK. Don't fight it. The important thing is to find your own pace, your own personal rhythm – a deeply satisfying experience. When you think about it, we spend most of our lives living by someone else's pace – our parents, our kids, our boss, our spouse. A walking trip is an opportunity to find and enjoy our own pace.

Comfort is the key once again. My pace will not be your pace. And your pace will vary from day to day, and from circumstance to circumstance.

Nonetheless, let me suggest three benchmark speeds:

> 1 mph = Slow
> 2 mph = Fast
> 3 mph = Too Fast

Let me also suggest *1 1/2 miles per hour* as a normal cruising speed, or "ordinary amble." This is an average pace that includes greeting people, taking photographs, admiring scenery, counting sheep, repairing broken stiles, retying your shoelaces, and so forth.

If you walk six hours a day at 1 1/2 miles per hour, you will cover nine miles – usually more than enough to take you to the next village. You can accomplish this easily by walking from 9 AM to noon, taking a break, and then walking from 1 to 4 PM. This will also get you to your destination well before the car traffic, so you will have plenty of time to find bed and breakfast.

A WALKER'S DAY

– Reviewing guidebook and marking map.	1 hr.
– Walking, including pauses, full stops and retracing of steps.	6
– Exploration of Roman roads, Celtic hillforts, Medieval castles, cathedrals, and other old rocks.	1–3
– Observation of scenic views, wildflowers, rare birds and red foxes, etc.	1–3
– Conversation with other walkers, B&B host, bank managers, children, pubkeepers, landowners, friendly cats & hungry sheep.	1–3
– Photography, general.	1
– Photography, of a special or fascinating subject, including self-portraits.	1
– Buying bikkies and sweets at the local newsagent or grocery shop.	1/2
– Eating, including tea and snacks.	2 1/2
– Map-reading, shoe-cleaning, path-upkeep, and other routine business of a British Footpath walker.	1 1/2
– Sleep, including naps beside the river.	8
– Journal writing and note taking.	1–3
– Time for toilet, bath and laundry.	1
– Getting lost, discovering you are lost, and deciding it's more fun to stay lost than use the official route anyway.	1 1/2

28-36 hrs.[*]

---

[*] Time can be elusive when walking in Britain! I invite you to make your own *Walker's Day* itinerary, to see if you can do any better. ☺!

Chapter 13

PHOTOGRAPHY

CAMERA, FILM, COST & SOURCES

CAMERAS vary from high-resolution Digital (expensive) to low-resolution Digital (poor quality and still expensive) to APS cameras (where you get a contact sheet vs negative strips) to traditional Single-Lens Reflex models (verstatile but bulky) to inexpensive Single-Use cameras (lightweight but not versatile).

If you are a serious photographer you may decide an SLR with interchangeable lens is best. If you are a novice you may want a fully automatic camera, which is smaller but also restricts the type of photographs you take.

I use a compact 35-millimeter camera which allows me to set the F-stop, shutter-speed and range-focus manually. The smallest 35mm cameras of this type I have found are the *Minox PL* and the *Olympus XA*. I have tried both, and found the Minox ingenious but too fiddly. I prefer the Olympus XA because of its convenience.

Special features of the XA include:

- The F-stop and shutter-speed are coordinated automatically. This eliminates certain special-effects, but for 99% of my needs this feature saves both time and trouble.

- You can adjust the range-focus and shutter-speed while looking through the viewfinder. This makes quick shots possible.

- No time limit on Time Exposures. The shutter stays open until enough light is admitted to create a photo. You can thus take a photo in a darkened room, or outdoors at night, without a flash.

- In addition to these unique features, the Olympus XA has the more typical features of a back-light switch, 10-second time-delay button (so you can get into the picture yourself) & flash attachment. Its chief drawback – which it shares with other compact cameras – is that you cannot attach special lenses.

Olympus no longer makes the XA, which has been replaced by more fully automatic but less versatile models. [As with Chrysler's slant-6 car engine, when something works *too* well, they stop making it because customers stop buying new models. Sigh!...] Fortunately, reconditioned XA's are fairly common, since professional photographers often use them as back-ups.

If you prefer a more fully automatic camera, try these:

- 35 MILLIMETER Pocket Cameras $150-250
  OLYMPUS *Stylus, Stlyus-Zoom & Stylus Epic*
  MINOLTA *Freedom Escort & Explorer*
  YASHICA *T4 Super*
  PENTAX *UC-1*

With these, F-stop range is limited (typically 3.5 to 16), time exposures are not always possible, and all the whirring and buzzing can be rather noisy. But they slip into your pocket, provide point-and-click ease of use, and produce high quality photos. All have a built-in flash and use lithium batteries.

The Minolta *Explorer* and Olympus *Stylus-Zoom* offer zoom lens (28 and 35 to 70mm, respectively). These make it easier to take close-ups of people without first standing on their shoelaces.

The Olympus *Stylus Epic* adds faster lens and shutter speeds, an improved viewfinder, and a waterproof* casing to its flagship pocket camera – already the best of its kind.

- ADVANCED PHOTO SYSTEM Pocket Cameras $300-500

Canon ELPH with a 30 to 60 mm equiv. zoom lens (and *ELPH Jr.*, no zoom lens) are winners among small APS cameras. They are the size and shape of a cigaret pack, with stainless steel bodies and high quality lens.

- DIGITAL Pocket Cameras $500-750

Olympus D-320L offers best value for its price of $700. 1024 x 768 resolution (vs 640 x 480 for comparables) at 24 bits/pixel color. A 2-Megabyte storage card holds 10 images in high-resolution mode; 30 in standard mode. Therefore you'll need to carry a hard drive to download images frequently, or else an awful lot of cameras.

Digital is poised to become the wave of the future, however. Hold on for the ride.

◊

FILM is heavy; so 36-exposure rolls are best. You do not need a lead shield to carry film in; airport X-rays will not harm ordinary film (400 speed or less). You can also ask the attendant to hand-check your film – although security regulations may prohibit this at times.

I use *200-speed* print film, Kodak's current standard, rather than 100-speed. The faster film permits photos indoors with normal lighting, and outdoors on dull days or at dusk – without a flash.

---

*I once dropped my XA into the River Irthing, yet it is still clicking happily along. So what's "new"?

You can also get 200-speed slide film. Keep in mind, however, that slide film is less forgiving than print film, and easier to over- or under-expose.

Finally, APS cameras use 24mm film. This produces *smaller* slides than 35 mm film, which makes it awkward to use both kinds of slides in the same slide show.

FLASH is not normally needed with 200-speed film.

COST of everything photographic is less in America than in Great Britain. Film that costs $5 here will cost $7 there. Buy it here! (Exception: *Boots* the Chemist sometimes has 3 for 2 specials on film – worth an inquiry.)

SOURCES for your reference:

A good *local* camera shop is your best bet for finding reconditioned cameras. Other sources include:

- *B&H Photo/Video/Audio*, New York. 1-800-947-6628. Request catalog. Good prices.

- *Camera World of Oregon*, Portland. 1-800-222-1557. Request catalog. Helpful service.

- *Jessop's Cameras* in Britain is a reliable chain with shops throughout the UK, including Oxford Street, London. They sometimes have cameras or equipment not yet available in the USA, and are worth a visit if you are a camera buff.

A CAMERA HOLSTER can be worth its weight in gold! A small "camera holster" will make spontaneous shots possible. And it is the spontaneous photos, just as it is the spontaneous events, that will be the most moving and most memorable.

Your camera holster does not need to be padded. But it *does* need to fit on your belt and provide quick, easy access to your camera. You should feel like Wyatt Earp, ready for a fast draw at any moment.

I cannot stress this too much. If you are unable to locate a ready-made pouch that works, then pay to have one custom-made, or make it yourself.

WHAT TO TAKE PHOTOS OF ?

That's easy ... Everything!

Everything, that is, except postcard shots of famous buildings, vistas, etc. Better and cheaper to purchase the postcard or slide from the gift shop. Save your film for things such as:

People – It is *people* who make most trips memorable, yet most often get left out of our photos. We are too shy, or they are too shy, or the camera isn't handy – always some excuse. If someone is camera-shy, ask him or her to take *your* photo first! Then you'll also end up with a few photos of yourself ... and after all, whose trip is it, anyway?

While they are taking your photograph, you have a chance to chat with them, get to know them a little, and let them get to know you a little. By the time they have taken a couple of photos of you, you are often talking about three or four topics, and they are no longer shy of your taking *their* photo.

Everyday Scenes – Seek out life's little asymmetries. It is the odd bits (not the polished and predictable ones) that make life interesting and valuable. The Cornishman sharpening his bread knife on a granite window sill, while his three-year-old son watches through the kitchen window. The Bath carpenter *handsawing* an oblong sandstone block to fit its niche in the façade of the Royal Crescent....

Such things capture the spirit of a place much more than the carefully prepared tourist events and sites.

Pub Signs – Whimsical or historical, cosy or comic, rustic or regal.... A fascinating study in themselves, pub signs (and pub names) often reflect local customs and local history.

Comic Signs – These abound, and in the most unlikely places. From the local church that advertises itself as full of "Strict and Particular" Baptists, to the homemade road sign warning traffic to slow down:

"10 mph – Dogs and Children *Everywhere!*"

Animal Shots – Shetland cows and quarrelsome seals, nesting puffins, playful seagulls and tiny cygnets, black cats, black swans and black sheep.... You will meet some curious critters on British footpaths. Of course, they think you're pretty curious, too. But they can't take your photo!

Shots for your Scrapbook – Expect to take a number of shots not because they are famous or artistic, but simply because they are part of your own story. Like the photograph of the sheep on the side of Cleeve Common, which I took from the bathtub of the Cleeve Hill Hotel. The scene has no redeeming artistic merit whatsoever. But every time I see it, I am back in that bathtub once again, reliving the relaxing end of a long day.

TELL A STORY!

Two things to remember:

- *Experiment Freely* – Don't be afraid to waste film. This can be difficult if you have Scottish blood (as I do). But go ahead! Spend a quarter and take the photo anyway, even if you think it won't turn out. I've been surprised more often than I can count.

- *Tell a Story* – One key difference between travel photography and general photography is that travel photography tells a story. Take notes as you take pictures if you wish; a word or two to remind you of the place or setting is often sufficient. Also, expect to collect some of your photos together in a Photo Album when you get home, both to remind yourself and to show friends.

Travel Photography tells a story. A paradox emerges here.... On the one hand, it is *your* story. You have total freedom to choose what to include or exclude. And yet – quite apart from your wishes in the matter – each journey also has *its own* story to tell. Pay attention and you will discover what that story is.

Experiment freely, and snap your photos in a relatively "uncensored" fashion. Don't stop to analyze why. When something attracts you, go ahead and take the picture. If you do this, then your journey will tell its own story through your uncensored photos. And later, when you spread out your photographs on the table before you, that story will surprise you with its subtlety and power.

Chapter 14

WALKING JOURNALS

A WALKING TRIP is a life in miniature.... Everything is intensified – the joys, the griefs, the pleasures, the disappointments. You can live through five years in a single day, a lifetime in a week!

This becomes is a special opportunity, psychologically and emotionally, to start fresh, to go through an entire "lifetime" – with a beginning, middle, and end – and to experience it as a *unified whole* that is greater than the sum of its parts.

That's where keeping a journal comes in ... your notes become your record of that life, intensely lived.

MATERIALS

Whatever works for you – looseleaf pages, notebooks, old candy wrappers. I use small orange MEMO BOOKS that cost about 50¢ and are available in Britain at chemist shops, bookstores and newsagents. These are stapled together rather than spiral bound, so they don't tear up my pockets. They fit easily into a shirt pocket, and one usually lasts a week or so. I often make brief notes about photographs in them, as well as general written notes at the end of the walking day.

◊

WHEN TO TAKE NOTES

There is no magic formula – although two schools of thought do emerge:

- Sit down on the nearest rock, and write it down *now*.
- Save it for tonight, with a pint and a packet of peanuts.

I've done both. I have paused during rush-hour on the London Underground to record a story or remark. I have also waited until the flight home to write something down, because there literally wasn't time before.... It has not seemed to matter. What has mattered is being fully tuned in *during* the experiences themselves.

Try to be flexible. Experiment to find out what works for you.

◊

WHAT TO WRITE ABOUT

For starters try these:

Place Names – Unfold the Landranger map of your area and begin to notice the place names. Many conceal tales of intrigue, humor and romance. Questions about these names can be a good way to meet the locals.

In the Lake District, mountains and lakes are given names such as *Catbells*, *Buttermere* and *Dollywaggon*. Cornwall is full of *Bollowalls*, *Gweeks* and *Quoits*. Yorkshire has its *Thwaites* and *Great Fryup Dales*. The Isle of Wight boasts *Baggywrinkles* and *Buddles Butt*. The Cotswolds offer delights such as *Twigworth* and *Tumpy Green*, *Old Sodbury* and *Upper Oddington*.

Imagine the fascinating pub discussions about the meaning and origin of these names!

Local Idioms – When someone says their "knickers are knackered" or calls you "toffee-nosed," perk up your ears and sharpen your pen. Ask questions. Take notes. You will enlarge your vocabulary, enrich your life, and who knows maybe make a new friend at the same time.

Comic Episodes – These are memories that will remain long after others have faded. Stories to tell your friends and your grandchildren. Like the time morning tea arrived in your B&B room before breakfast ... and before you were dressed!

Special People – The German student who shared her breakfast with you. The 86-year-old Welshman walking the Pembrokeshire Coast Path with his great grandson. The homesick Scot playing his bagpipes in the Lake District. Four-year-old Anna, pushing her own pram on the River Thames towpath. James and Sarah from Kent, who've visited their favorite spot on the South Downs each May for the past 22 years. Arthur, puffing his pipe furiously as he declares Roman roads in his native Leiscestershire still display their original chariot ruts. Colin, whose wife dropped him off on top of the North York Moors after an argument and told him to walk back. He did ... with you!

It is the *people,* in the end, who will turn your trip into a journey of the spirit as well as the leg muscles. Just a few notes will bring back their stories.

Literary, Historical & Geological Notes Along the Way.

Whatever your interests – trees, mushrooms, birds, wildflowers, English Civil War Society, cathedrals, stone circles, etc. – you will find grist for your mill (and notes for your journal) along the footpath.

Reflections – If you are philosophically inclined at all, a walking trip will surprise you with new perspectives, sudden insights, and unexpected gestalts. Take a few notes to remind yourself what life feels like outside Plato's cave.

Drawings – Even if you "can't draw," give it a try anyway. A rough sketch of a face or special landscape will be enough to remind you of the whole experience for years to come.

I once read it usually takes two days to "unwind" when you go on vacation, while the "afterglow" (if you are lucky) can last up to a week....

With a walking trip to England, your unwind time can be virtually instantaneous. After a short train ride, you can often begin walking the day you arrive. (The Sussex Border Path follows the boundary of Gatwick Airport, and one of these days I am going to walk out of the airport!)

As for the afterglow, it can last for the rest of your life.

◊

A walking trip is a life in miniature ... and your walking journals will allow you to relive that life, again and again.

Chapter 15

THE COUNTRY CODE

WHEN WE WALK in Britain, we are guests ... and these are the rules. England is densely populated, and the countryside is so unspoilt because people follow the Country Code:

> Guard against risk of fire. (Don't start fires.)
> Fasten all gates.
> Keep dogs under close control.
> Keep to paths across farmland.
> Avoid damaging fences, hedges and walls.
> Leave no litter.
> Safeguard water supplies.
> Protect wildlife, plants and trees.
> Go carefully on country roads.
> Respect the life of the countryside.

America has "parks and trails," England has "country-side and access." The difference is subtle and profound. In Britain, no rigid distinctions exist among farmland, parkland and wilderness. It is all *countryside*, woven together by 120,000 miles of public footpaths.

Thus, when you are walking in England, treat the land as if it belonged to someone else, because it does. Treat it as if it belonged to *you* ... because it also does.

Do this, and both land and people will become your friends. And you will have joined the unspoken fellowship of the footpath.

Congratulations!

Epilogue

HOW CAN I TELL YOU?

PERHAPS I HAVE conveyed something of the beauty, history, and people of England. And how accessible they all are if you go with the attitude of a fellow-traveler rather than simply as a tourist.

But this is a matter ultimately beyond words to convey.

How can I "tell" you about walking across the South Downs, or through the Yorkshire Dales – where history stalks you like a prey until it is felt in the blood, like some strange yet intimate companion from your own childhood?

How can I "tell" you the feeling of soaking your feet in the River Thames – *Father Thames* as they call it – or of coming suddenly upon a field of poppies or a clump of edelweiss daisies that have just opened their petals that morning, as if all for you?

How can I "tell" you the feeling when a local villager offers you a cup of tea as you walk past his or her village? Or a scrap of mending wool to darn your sweater?

I cannot "tell" you about these things in the end. You have to experience them for yourself. And when you do go – whether it is next week, or next year, or in the next ten years – you *will* experience them for yourself.

And if you walk lightly amid the noise and haste, there will be moments when you feel utterly, naively alive.... And that, in the end, is what it's all about.

FOOTPATH

Appendix A

SCOTLAND

SCOTLAND, as the Scots will quickly remind you, is *not* England. Nor does it much resemble other Celtic corners of the world – such as Ireland, Wales, Brittany and Cornwall – but that is another story. The point here is that Scotland is different from England – a world unto itself, and quite happy to have it that way.

England has always had political aspirations toward Scotland. Kings from Edward I to Henry VII have even enlisted the Arthurian legend to bolster their Scottish claims. The Romans knew better. They built their Antonine and Hadrian's Walls more for political than military purposes, and otherwise left the Picts and Scots alone. Only after the bloody Battle of Bannockburn in 1314 (which the English call "Battle of the Bogs") did Anglo-Saxon England adopt the same policy as the Romans. A policy which – despite an official "union of crowns" in 1603 and "union of parliaments" in 1707 – has continued ever since.

Today a grudging respect exists between the two peoples. The English at times see their northern neighbors as pinch-penny, over-sexed anarchists – but they also admire the Scots for their practical genius (the Industrial Revolution was led by Scottish engineers), their military prowess (the Queen's crack troops are the Scots Guards), and their independent spirit.

The Scots, in turn, tend to consider their southern neighbors to be over-cautious, duplicitous snobs. Yet they admire the English for their artistic, political, and social achievements – things such as English literature, the Empire, and the BBC. Scots also acknowledge the English sense of fair play, skill at building community, and ability to laugh at themselves.

It is, however, an uneasy partnership, and the wind-swept uplands of the Cheviot Hills serve as a strategic geographical border between Scotland and England. The easy victory of the 1997 "devolution" vote offers a gentle reminder of these underlying feelings.

South of the border, the English are usually mildly surprised to learn that such a nice person as YOU could be from such a boisterous place as America.... Scots, on the other hand, often sense an immediate kinship with Americans, and tend to assume you share their generosity of spirit and passionate love of freedom.

The English are *eccentric*; the Scots are *independent*.

Americans, on balance, are more like their Scottish than their English cousins.

◊

Walking in Scotland is thus – not surprisingly – a rather different experience than walking in England. A few of those differences include:

(1) There are no laws of trespass in Scotland!... If you do no damage, you are free to go where you will. This might seem a great advantage, but is not as friendly to ramblers as first appears. True, there is a sort of utopian freedom to roam. But lack of official trespass also means lack of official "rights-of-way". Maps of Scotland do not have the friendly little red dashes indicating footpaths, which walkers in England have come to love and rely upon.

This suits many Scottish ramblers just fine. They enjoy nothing better than to strap on their rucksacks and disappear into the hills for a long weekend. What does it matter that there are no marked trails, when you prefer to make your own anyway? But this is more like hiking in America – requiring boots, tent, sleeping bag and food for the journey.

Unless you have Scottish relatives, you might prefer to save your money and go hiking in the Cascades or Appalachians instead.

(2) Finding Bed & Breakfast can be a problem at times because of sparse population. Scotland is almost as large as England, but there are only five million Scots, compared to fifty-five million English. Towns and villages are thus farther apart than their English counterparts.

(3) The *relative* scarcity of history is a third important difference between walking in Scotland and England. The Scottish people do have a rich history of their own, and no history buff will be disappointed. But Scottish history simply cannot compete with the density and variety of English history. Again this is mostly a matter of relative population. Fewer people mean less history. And longer walks between historical sites.

As a rule then, walking in Scotland is more like hiking in America. Except for the absence of trespassing laws, that is. Also there is a fourth point wherein Scotland is like neither America nor England....

(4) Midges (Ahem!) – If America has mosquitoes, and England has no significant insects for walkers to deal with (unless you count seagulls), Scotland cannot escape its reputation for *midges*. Books have been written on midges. Volcanic Celtic oaths have been sworn, and lavish University grants squandered trying to get rid of the wee beasties.

Midges, in brief, are tiny Scottish super-gnats. they do not buzz; they bite. When several dozen bite you at the same time, you wonder why you complained about the seagulls and mosquitoes.

Fortunately, midges thrive only during July and August when conditions are relatively warm and damp. And even then, mostly in isolated areas like Rannoch Moor, where extensive boglands serve as breeding grounds.

Therefore, the best advice is don't go wandering across the Highlands in July and August. During other months, you should have no problem. September is usually good, when purple heather will cheer you along the way.

◊

West Highland Way*

The *West Highland Way* is a remarkable exception to most general rules about walking in Scotland. Thanks to the hard work of the National Park Service and dedicated volunteers, there now exists a waymarked path (for all practical purposes like an English right-of-way) from the outskirts of Glasgow to Fort William.

The route follows old drover's trails, canal towpaths, and military roads into the heart of the Highlands – past romantic Loch Lomond, historic Glencoe (famous for its massacre), and *pre*historic Rannoch Moor (within sight of Ian Fleming's Scottish estate).

Farmhouses, Villages, Scottish Youth Hostels (among the best in the world) and Highland Hotels (uniquely Scottish and reasonably priced) provide ample accommodation in route. You even get free samples of Scottish Malt Whisky at distilleries along the way!

---

*Guidebook and B&B list available from *British Footpaths.*

Some Scottish walkers consider the West Highland Way too tame for their taste. But it remains the best maintained and most accessible Long Distance Path in Scotland. And after you have finished trekking beside Rannoch Moor, or crossing the Devil's Staircase to reach Kinlochleven, you will have achieved a genuine taste of the Highlands ... without risking life and limb to do it.

◊

Fife Coast Path*

The *Fife Coast Path* – Edinburgh to St Andrews – has become a second accessible Long Distance Path in Scotland. It remains an "unofficial" route. But ramblers have been working with planning commissions and landowners to establish links between existing paths along a coast that locals have loved and walked for hundreds of years. A few negotiations remain but work is largely complete, and the *Fife Coast Path* has already begun to emerge as Edinburgh's alternative to Glasgow's *West Highland Way*.

The *Fife Coast Path* crosses the Forth Bridge and traces the historic Fife coast past the ruined castles, ancient caves and picturesque fishing villages of East Neuk (home of the original Robinson Crusoe), to reach the ancient birthplace of Golf itself – where you can contemplate the tangled skein of Scottish history as you stroll *unencumbered* beside the famous "Road Hole," or walk across the little stone bridge over Swilken Burn – just as Old Tom Morris himself might have done. The little bridge has been there 300 years, since Mary Queen of Scots gave the land on which the Old Course was built to the people of St Andrews.

---

*For information on the Fife Coast Path (and a free B&B list) write to *British Footpaths*, 914 Mason, Bellingham, WA 98225.

Explore the mysterious yet accessible Kingdom of Fife on foot, and you may begin to understand a thing or two about the Scottish people that even Glasgow and the West Highland Way won't teach you.

Other Scottish LDP's
None of Scotland's other Long Distance Paths – official or unofficial – is half as accessible as the West Highland Way and Fife Coast Path. The *Speyside Walk* is hard to get to and from. The *Southern Upland Way* is a much longer walk over much less populated territory. The *Great Glen Path* – Fort William to Inverness – has promise, but is still in the planning stage. See map and notes on page 90.

Day Walks in Scotland
Discovering accessible Day Walks in Scotland presents similar problems, because of rough terrain and distance between villages. The *Trossachs* region (NE of Glasgow; NW of Edinburgh) is one of the few areas for day walks that does not require special experience or stamina, although you will need a car to get there. Stirling, Aberfoyle and Callander all make good centers for a walking holiday in the Trossachs.

North-West Scotland

Finally, if you would like to venture into the Scottish "outback," to explore the northwest coast above Ullapool, I cannot recommend going it alone.... This is starkly beautiful but extremely isolated mountainous terrain. It is the one place in Britain where I would urge you to join a group tour. Either ask a Scottish relative to accompany you, or enlist the aid of a local guide such as Andrew Bluefield.

Andrew lives in Ullapool, and leads guided walks into these otherwise inaccessible areas. Contact him through *NorthWest Frontiers*, Strathkanaird, Ullapool, Ross-shire, Scotland (Tel 01854-666229).

Scottish Natural Heritage

For further information about walking in Scotland, write the staff at Scottish Natural Heritage, Battleby, Redgorton, Perth, Scotland PH1 3EW. They are quite helpful, within the limits of their official knowledge.

The Scottish people, however, are seldom limited by anything "official." And when you meet them on your walking trip, you will find a personal warmth and hospitality that would impress ... even the English!

Travel to Scotland

Save both time and money by flying directly to Scotland. The new Glasgow Airport is a 20-minute bus ride from the center of Glasgow, which recently won the *European City of Culture* award. Glasgow is no longer "Edinburgh's unlovely sister" and will repay a lingering visit before or after your walk.

Appendix B

DAY WALKS

GREAT BRITAIN is a nation of walkers.... Hence the large number of day walks accessible to ordinary people. These walks are often, though by no means always, found in Britain's national parks – such as the Lake District, Yorkshire Dales, or Exmoor.

Favorite areas for day walks include: (Map overleaf)

Cornwall
Cotswolds
Devon
Dorset
East Anglia (Norfolk)
Exmoor
Isle of Wight
Kent
Lake District
London
Northumberland
North York Moors
Pembrokeshire (Wales)
Snowdonia (Wales)
Sussex
Trossachs (Scotland)
Yorkshire Dales

FAVORITE AREAS FOR DAY WALKS

Day Walk Guides & Sources

Day-walk guidebooks proliferate in England, though they are not always easy to find, and they vary widely in quality, cost and ease of use.

Those likely to be available in the U.S. include:

- *Book of Country Walks; Walks & Tours; Village Walks* (O-S/AA) are three large-format, loose-leaf volumes with removable pages. Well-done, but quite expensive. (Jointly published by Ordnance Survey [O-S] and the Automobile Association of Great Britain [AA]).

- *Pathfinder Guides*+ (O-S/Jarrold) to walks in selected areas of Britain are less expensive and generally good value, but do vary quite a bit from volume to volume. My favorites cover the Yorkshire Dales, Isle of Wight, Exmoor, Pembrokeshire, and Lake District.

- *Best of Britain's Countryside* by Bill and Gwen North (The Mountaineers). These two "walk & drive" guides are among the few guides published in America. Sadly, the frenetic pace rather undercuts the point of being in the countryside in the first place.

◊

If you would like more information about particular day walks or recommended guidebooks, you might contact the *British Tourist Authority* (551-Fifth Ave, NY, NY 10019 Tel 212-986-2200), or *Ramblers Association* (1/5 Wandsworth Rd, London, England SW8 2XX Tel (171-582-6878).

Both publish helpful brochures, and are worth asking. Be aware of their institutional nature, however, and if you receive a personal answer from someone who has actually been on the walks they recommend, consider it a bonus.

+Pathfinder Guides are available from *British Footpaths*, 914 Mason, Bellingham, WA 98225. Tel 360-671-1217.

◊

A different kind of source (with a different kind of bias) is *British Footpath Bibliography: An Annotated Guide to Guidebooks,* by R. Hayward, which has a separate section on each region listed on page 83. This book is limited to the experience of the author, but has the advantage of sharing personal knowledge and enthusiasm.

A smaller companion volume, *British Footpath Sampler,* describes 28 favorite day walks chosen from Hayward's own experience. These walks are all accessible by public transport, and are chosen for their historic as well as scenic interest. Most are circular, and two or more walks can be done from each town or village.

The *Sampler* also suggests a dozen "easy" long distance paths that can be enjoyed by ordinary ramblers.

◊

The best advice of all invariably comes from the local people themselves. Thus if the guidebooks do not spark your imagination, then just go ... and ask the locals (beginning with your Bed & Breakfast host and local pubkeeper) about *their* favorite day walks.

Enjoy!

Appendix C

LONG DISTANCE PATHS

A LONG DISTANCE PATH (LDP) is a continuous right-of-way through the countryside. These usually lead from village to village and avoid large urban areas. They can be as short as 20 miles or as long as 500 miles, but most are between 50 and 150 miles and can be walked in one or two weeks by the average walker.

These can be river walks, ridge ways, or coast paths. Others defy conventional categories. Many LDP's are as much a walk through time as through distance. They often invite us to people valleys, villages and pubs with the ghosts of previous centuries. Or listen for echoes of our own ancestors, who toiled and fought and loved upon those very hillsides.

◊

To walk in Britain is, on the one hand, an exercise in self-sufficiency and an invitation to self-knowledge. Yet it is also an adventure in experiencing our essential *connectedness* with others – both past and present – who have shared our path. Pilgrims, explorers and adventurers ... fugitives, refugees and writers ... even fellow-tourists ... all accompany us along the ancient trackways and down the country lanes.

As a walker of British footpaths, you may often find yourself a solitary wanderer, but you will seldom feel lonely.

What follows is a map of selected LDP's, intended to introduce rather than exhaust possibilities.

LONG DISTANCE PATHS
OF
ENGLAND & WALES

Key to Map

1. South West Way* (combines 2,3,4 & 5)
2. Somerset and North Devon Coast Path*
3. Cornwall Coast Path*†
4. South Devon Coast Path*†
5. Dorset Coast Path*†
6. Two Moors Way
7. Cotswold Way†
8. Thames Walk*†
9. Ridgeway Path*
10. Wayfarer's Way
11. Isle of Wight Coastal Path†
12. South Downs Way*†
13. North Downs Way / Pilgrims Way*†
14. Wealdway
15. Saxon Shore Way
16. Pembrokeshire Coast Path*†
17. Glyndwr's Way
18. Offa's Dyke Path*
19. Wye Valley Walk
20. Shropshire Way
21. Peddar's Way and Norfolk Coast Path*†
22. Viking Way
23. Wolds Way*
24. Cleveland Way*
25. Three Dales Way†
26. Dales Way
27. Cumbria Way
28. Coast to Coast Walk†
29. Hadrian's Wall Walk†
30. Pennine Way*

---

* "Official" LDP's.

† Guidebooks (and B&B lists) for these paths available from *British Footpaths* 914 Mason, Bellingham WA 98225.

LONG DISTANCE PATHS
OF
SCOTLAND

Key to Map

31. Southern Upland Way*
32. West Highland Way*†
33. Speyside Walk
34. Great Glen Path (proposed)
35. Fife Coast Path†

---

* "Official" LDP's.

† Guidebook and B&B list available from *British Footpaths.*

Most paths have three or four different guidebooks of varying cost and quality. A series of *National Trail Guides* exists for the fifteen or so "official" LDP's, but these are not always the best value.

◊

References:

- *National Trust Book of Long Walks*, by Adam Nicolson (Pan/Crown Books). The best general book about Britain's long distance paths. Available in American bookstores. About $20.

- *Long Distance Walker's Handbook*, Barbara Blatchford (A & C Black, Ltd.). The most comprehensive list of Long Distance Paths as well as their guidebooks. Non-evaluative. About £12 ($20) postpaid.

- *British Footpath Bibliography: An Annotated Guide to Guidebooks,* by Richard Hayward (British Footpaths). Critiques guidebooks for over 30 LDP's, based on the author's own experience. $10 postpaid.

- *British Footpath Sampler*, by Richard Hayward (British Footpaths). Briefly describes a dozen "easy" LDP's – accessible to anyone willing to carry an 8 to 10 lb. pack, and go at his or her own pace. $5 postpaid.

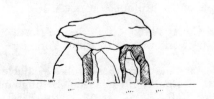

— WHERE TO BEGIN —

1. **Isle of Wight Coast Path** – Easy walk around the entire island, called the "Garden of England" and "England in Miniature."

2. **A Pilgrims Way** – Follow Chaucer through the apple orchards and hop fields of Kent, from Rochester to Canterbury, via Leeds Castle and Wye.

3. **Cornwall Coast Path** – Lands End to Lizard Point. An intensely Celtic corner of Britain, haunted by Arthurian sites. Visit Penzance & St Michael's Mount.

4. **South Downs Way** – Sussex will bewitch you with the beauty of her subtle slopes and sudden valleys. Saxon villages, Celtic hillforts, and Roman villas.

5. **Pembrokeshire Coast Path** – Fishguard to Little Haven. Walk around the coast of South Wales, blanketed with wildflowers each spring.

6. **Cotswold Way** – Through the Shire of J.R.R. Tolkien's imagination. Stride among Stone-age long barrows and thatched villages, from Chipping Campden to Bath.

7. **Three Dales Way** – Riverside walk among the buttercup meadows & small stone villages of the Yorkshire Dales.

8. **Hadrian's Wall Walk** – Cumbria and Northumberland. The Romans built it to keep the Scots on *their* side of the border. After 2000 years, the Wall still beckons....

9. **West Highland Way** – From the shores of Loch Lomond to the foot of Ben Nevis. There is no better way to meet the people of this unique country.

10. **Coast to Coast Walk** – Irish Sea to North Sea, via the Lake District and James Herriot's Yorkshire.

Guides and maps for these walks available from *British Footpaths*, 914 Mason, Bellingham WA 98225. Call (360) 671-1217 for free catalog.

Appendix D

BRITISH VOCABULARY
USEFUL TO WALKERS

OUTDOORS

COUNTRYSIDE – Everything outside the city, town or village is *countryside*. This is multi-use land which includes farmland, parkland and wilderness.

HEDGEROW – A row of intertwined "bushes" typically used as a field boundary. The Saxons preferred hawthorn; Exmoor has beech tree hedges. Medieval footpaths often followed the line of hedgerows, which would provide shade for tired walkers and a habitat for birds, butterflies, and insects. Hedgerows are found mostly in Southern England, while stone walls serve similar functions in the North. The art of "laying a hedge" is a dying skill, but where hedgerows still exist they continue to serve their original purpose.

TWITTEN – A pedestrian-only pathway in a town or village. Used chiefly in Southeast England, but understood throughout the country. Numerous local names exist for this sort of informal urban pathway. Some of these include *Ginnell* (West Yorkshire), *Wynd* (North Yorkshire), *Opie* (Cornwall), *Jigger* or *Jowler* (Liverpool), *Twitchels* (Oxfordshire), and *Drang* (South Wales). Compile your own list; have fun.

SNICKET – A makeshift opening through a thicket, or hedgerow. Think of it as a "rural twitten."

SPINNEY – A double row of trees planted as a field boundary, usually with a footpath between the rows.

STILE – An arrangement of steps or a deliberate gap, allowing people but not animals to climb a fence or wall. Usually made of wood or stone. Stiles come in various forms – step stiles, ladder stiles, gap stiles and squeeze stiles. Even mechanical stiles with ingenious weighted levers or bootsole hinges. But I have yet to see a stile that operates by computer command.

PLINTH – Small concrete waymarker, especially in the South of England.

WEALD – Woodland (South).

DOWN – Rolling open hills, with grass (South).

FELL – Open rolling hills with grass growing on them, in the North of England. Usually higher and somewhat more rugged than a "down" in the South of England, but otherwise similar.

DALE – Valley (North). *Yorkshire Dales*, etc.

TARN – Small lake (North). Especially in Lake District.

TARNLET – A small tarn.

BECK –A stream or small river (North).

GILL – A stream or small river, in a ravine (North).

FORCE – Waterfall.

WATERFALL – Rapids.

CAIRN – (1) Pile of stones to mark the summit or the line of the footpath on a mountain or fell. (2) Ancient grave, consisting of a pile of stones originally covered with earth and grass.

TUMULUS – Usually an ancient gravesite (on maps).

TRIG POINT – "Trigonometric" cement marker originally used by mapmakers to indicate the summit of a hill. More useful today as landmarks or waymarks.

WOLDS – Hills (Cots*wolds*, Yorkshire *Wolds*, etc.).

BACK GARDEN – Back yard. Called a *garden* because the assumption is there will be more flowers than grass.

GREEN – Park.

R.U.P.P. – Road Used as Public Path. Usually a small country road, with little traffic.

VERGE – Shoulder of a road.

LAY-BY – Paved shoulder of a road, or roadside turnout.

VILLAGE AND URBAN LIFE

POSTE RESTANTE – General Delivery.

LEFT LUGGAGE – A locker or room with attendants where you can check parcels or luggage for a per-hour or per-day fee. Most useful.

UNDERGROUND or TUBE – Subway.

SUBWAY – A pedestrian underpass.

PAVEMENT – A sidewalk.

MOTORWAY – Freeway with several lanes and limited access. Similar to U.S. Interstate Highway.

DUAL CARRIAGEWAY – Divided highway.

ROUNDABOUT – Traffic circle.

FLYOVER – Overpass.

DIVERSION – Detour.

LORRY – Truck.

PETROL – Gasoline.

BOOT – Trunk of a car.

BONNET – Hood of a car.

BUS – Local or Intracity bus.

COACH – Intercity bus.

RAILWAY STATION – Train station.

TOILET – Restroom.

LOO – Toilet or john. Even the Queen Mother calls it "the loo" in England. So *loo*sen up!

BATHROOM – Room with a bathtub, but not necessarily with a toilet.

PORTALOO – Portable toilet.

ZEBRA CROSSING – Pedestrian crosswalk. (Pronounced "zebb-ra.")

NEWSAGENT – Shop that sells newspapers, snack food, stationery supplies, bandaids, local maps and guides, tobacco, candy, etc.

QUEUE – Line of people waiting their turn at a grocery shop, bus stop, theater, etc.

POST BOX (or POSTING BOX) – Mail box for mailing letters.

TO RING (GIVE SOMEONE A RING) – To telephone.

TO CALL – To visit in person.

FLAT – Apartment.

TO LET – To rent (an apartment).

TO HIRE – To rent (a bicycle or car).

DUSTBIN or RUBBISH BIN – Trash can.

JUMBLE SALE – Rummage sale.

GENERAL

RETURN – Round trip ticket on train, bus or airplane.

SINGLE – One-way ticket.

RUCKSACK – Backpack.

TO GO ON HOLIDAY – To take a vacation.

DUBBIN – To oil or polish shoes or boots (verb). The oil or polish itself (noun).

DOCTOR'S SURGERY – Doctor's office.

RUBBER – Eraser.

KNACKERED – Tired. Pooped. Whacked.

TO KNOCK YOU UP IN THE MORNING – To wake you up.

HALF-ELEVEN (etc.) – Half *past* eleven o'clock.

PHOTO – As in "Would you please take a photo of me?' or "Could I please take your photo?" In England a *picture* is something you draw or paint, not something you take with a camera.

FOOD

BISCUITS – Cookies.

BIKKIES – Cookies (diminutive).

CRISPS – Potato Chips.

CHIPS – Chunky French Fries.

ORANGE LOLLY – Orange popsicle.

ORANGE FIZZY – Carbonated orange drink.

ORANGE SQUASH – Non-carbonated orange drink.

LAGER – Resembles American beer, drunk cold.

BITTER – Ordinary English beer, usually drunk at room temperature.

ALE – Somewhat richer and sweeter than "bitter." Try Newcastle Brown Ale.

STOUT – Densest of all English beers. Try Mackeson's.

SHANDY – Beer-and-lemonade drink. An acquired taste.

SCRUMPY – West Country hard cider (Somerset and Devon). Packs a wallop!

PUDDING or SWEET(S) – Dessert.

JAM – Preserves.

JELLY – Gelatin.

HORLICKS – Malty hot drink at bedtime. Similar to Ovaltine. Called the "food drink of the night." Said to prevent "night starvation."

BAG – Small bag.

SACK – Large bag.

SERVIETTE – Table napkin.

CLOTHING

JUMPER – Sweater. "Woolly jumper" = wool sweater.

KNEE BREECHES – Knickerbockers or knickers.

KNICKERS – Women's underpants.

PANTS – Men's underpants.

TROUSERS – Pants or slacks.

VEST – Undershirt.

TIGHTS – Nylons.

PLIMSOLLS – Sneakers.

TRAINERS – Running shoes.

AT THE CHEMIST SHOP

CHEMIST – Pharmacy or drugstore; Pharmacist.

PLASTER – Bandaid.

RALJAX – *Bengué (BenGay)*. Wintergreen ointment for sprains and strains.

SELLOTAPE – Scotch Tape.

TORCH – Flashlight.

SURGICAL SPIRIT – Rubbing alcohol.

FACE CLOTH – Washcloth.

BIRO – Ballpoint pen.

British Footpath Titles
– Richard Hayward –

BRITISH FOOTPATH HANDBOOK $10 postpaid
Independent Walking Tours of England, Wales, Scotland
How to do-it-yourself with an 8-lb pack & $35 a day.
Save on airfares, trains, pubs, food, photography,
postage and more. Distills knowledge gleaned from
twenty years of slow rambling and fast thinking.

BRITISH FOOTPATH BIBLIOGRAPHY $10 postpaid
Annotated Guide to Guidebooks
Guides & maps vary in quality, cost and emphasis.
This book advises which ones work best, and why.
Covers 30+ Long Distance Paths, plus day walks.
Sources for guidebooks, maps and *B&B Lists*.

BRITISH FOOTPATH SAMPLER $5 postpaid
Favorite Day Walks & Easy Long Distance Paths
28 day walks and 12 LDP's – *accessible* to ordinary
ramblers. If you're sweating or shivering while walking in Britain, then you're doing something wrong.

THE COTSWOLD WAY
A Walk Through Middle-Earth $9 postpaid
Story of a walk through the Shire of J.R.R. Tolkien's
imagination – from Bath to Chipping Campden. Visit
Broadway Tower & Hetty Pegler's Tump.... Gives you
a "feel" for doing it yourself, getting lost, finding your
own pace, and meeting the people.

A COAST TO COAST WALK
Serendipitous Journey Across England $9 postpaid
Story of a walk from the Irish Sea to the North Sea,
via the Lake District & Yorkshire. Suggests detours
and alternate routes – around the boggy bits, along
Roman roads, and into favorite pubs.

CORNWALL COAST PATH GUIDE
Lands End to Lizard Point $9 postpaid
The most accessible stretch of the Cornwall coast.
Visit Penzance and St. Michael's Mount. Includes
B&B list and maps, notes on pubs, history, geology
and wildlife, short cuts and alternate routes.

British Footpath Guides (continued)

A PILGRIM'S WAY GUIDE

A Week's Walk in Kent $9 postpaid

Follow Chaucer through the apple orchards and hopfields of Kent – from Rochester to Leeds Castle and Canterbury. B&B lists, pub notes, maps, etc.

HADRIAN'S WALL WALK GUIDE

A Journey Through Time $9 postpaid

Hadrian's Wall may in fact be Hadrian's Folly, but it is a folly that seizes our imaginations and haunts our dreams. B&B lists, pub notes, maps, etc.

THREE DALES WAY GUIDE

Buttercups and Drystone Walls $9 postpaid

Stroll among buttercup meadows and stone villages, waterfalls and wildflowers in the Yorkshire Dales. B&B lists, pub notes, maps, etc.

PEMBROKESHIRE COAST PATH GUIDE

Of Dragons and Wildflowers $9 postpaid

Explore the coast of South Wales, blanketed with wildflowers each spring. Visit a Celtic village and St David's Cathedral. B&B lists, pub notes, maps, etc.

ISLE OF WIGHT COAST PATH GUIDE

England in Miniature $9 postpaid

Easy walk around the entire island, famous for dinosaur bones and white cliffs, thatched villages and special pubs, Osborne House and Carisbrooke Castle. B&B lists, pub notes, maps, etc.

FIFE COAST PATH GUIDE

Edinburgh to St Andrews $9 postpaid

Explore Scottish castles & East Neuk fishing villages of Anstruther, Pittenweem and Crail, as you explore the shy, serendipitous kingdom of Fife, birthplace of golf. B&B lists, pub notes, maps, etc.

All titles may be ordered from:

British Footpaths
914 Mason, Bellingham, WA 98225
(360) 671-1217